I0022221

# Development Finance Institutions

## Measuring Their Subsidy

# Development Finance Institutions

## *Measuring Their Subsidy*

Mark Schreiner
Jacob Yaron

THE WORLD BANK
WASHINGTON, D.C.

Copyright © 2001 The International Bank for Reconstruction
and Development/THE WORLD BANK
1818 H Street, N.W.
Washington, D.C. 20433, USA

All rights reserved
Manufactured in the United States of America
First printing October 2001
1 2 3 4  04 03 02 01

The findings, interpretations, and conclusions expressed in this book are entirely those
of the authors and should not be attributed in any manner to the World Bank, to its affil-
iated organizations, or to members of its Board of Executive Directors or the countries
they represent. The World Bank does not guarantee the accuracy of the data included
in this publication and accepts no responsibility for any consequence of their use.

The material in this publication is copyrighted. The World Bank encourages dis-
semination of its work and will normally grant permission to reproduce portions of
the work promptly.

Permission to *photocopy* items for internal or personal use, for the internal or personal use of specific clients, or for educational classroom use is granted by the World
Bank, provided that the appropriate fee is paid directly to the Copyright Clearance
Center, Inc., 222 Rosewood Drive, Danvers, MA 01923, USA; telephone 978-750-8400,
fax 978-750-4470. Please contact the Copyright Clearance Center before photocopying
items.

For permission to *reprint* individual articles or chapters, please fax a request with
complete information to the Republication Department, Copyright Clearance Center,
fax 978-750-4470.

All other queries on rights and licenses should be addressed to the Office of the
Publisher, World Bank, at the address above or faxed to 202-522-2422.

Cover photo credit: Curt Carnemark, 1994; Morocco
Cover background: Tomas Sennett, undated; Brazil

**Library of Congress Cataloging-in-Publication Data**

Schreiner, Mark, 1969–
    Development finance institutions : measuring their subsidy / Mark Schreiner,
    Jacob Yaron.
       p.    cm.  —  (Directions in development)
    Includes bibliographical references.
    ISBN 0-8213-4984-8
       1. Development credit corporations.    2. Development banks.    3. Subsidies.
    4. Externalities (Economics)    I. Yaron, Jacob.  II. Title.    III. Series.

    HG3726 .S34   2001
    332.2'8—dc21                                                    2001045424

# Contents

**Tables**

**Figures**

**Boxes**

# Abstract

Measures of the social cost of development finance institutions (DFIs) that receive public funds help to check whether DFIs are good uses of public funds. Public funds are well-spent—and social welfare is improved—if the social benefit of a DFI exceeds the social cost. The term *development finance institution* encompasses not only government development banks but also thousands of nongovernmental microfinance organizations worldwide that use matching grants to attempt to promote community development, decentralization of power, and local empowerment. This monograph describes the measurement of costs but not of benefits, but even without precise knowledge of benefits, knowledge of costs can help to spend funds well. It is less expensive to measure costs than benefits, and "cost calculations can provide a useful 'reality check' on proposed interventions. Whatever the true [unknown] size of external benefits, the government must judge that at a minimum the external benefit exceeds this cost for the intervention to be worth undertaking" (Devarajan, Squire, and Suthiwart-Narueput 1997, p. 40).

This monograph presents two measures of social cost. The first is the Subsidy Dependence Index (SDI). The SDI does not discount flows, so it works best in short time frames or when the rate of time preference is low. The SDI is the ratio of subsidy received to revenue from loans. *Subsidy* is defined as the social cost of the public funds used to run a DFI. The measure of subsidy can also be used to adjust common measures of financial performance such as Return on Equity (ROE) or Return on Assets (ROA).

The second measure is the Net Present Cost to Society ($NPC_S$). Like standard present-value measures, the $NPC_S$ discounts cash flows and works in any time frame.

The SDI and the $NPC_S$ are useful because common financial ratios—such as ROE—may hide the true performance of DFIs because their measures of cost may not reflect social opportunity costs. The SDI and the $NPC_S$ shift the paradigm from reported (accounting) costs—much of which are routinely subsidized—to opportunity (economic) costs. The two measures proposed here use standard tools of project analysis to answer questions from the point of view of society. The questions and answers also matter to governments and donors who care about sustainability. A *sustainable* DFI can meet its goals now and in the long term. Sustainability improves social welfare if the consequent long-term increase in the length, breadth, scope, and quality of outreach compensate for the short-term increases in costs shifted to the target group. By definition, a *subsidy-independent* DFI has no social cost in financial terms.

The SDI and the $NPC_S$ are simple tools, and their results are only as good as their data and assumptions. Like other yardsticks, they help to establish benchmarks, chart trends, and compare a DFI with peers with identical clients and services.

The measurement of the social cost of public DFIs matters because funds earmarked for development are scarce. Subsidies for DFIs are not bad unless they could improve social welfare more somewhere else. The measurement of social cost as described in this monograph is a first step toward wiser use of public funds.

# Acknowledgments

We are thankful for comments from Stephanie Charitonenko, Carlos Cuevas, Douglas Graham, Michael Lyne, Jonathan Morduch, Sergio Navajas, Glenn Pederson, Richard Rosenberg, Michael Sherraden, and participants in seminars at The Ohio State University. The opinions expressed are not necessarily those of Washington University in St. Louis nor of the World Bank.

# Glossary of Acronyms

| | |
|---|---|
| BancoSol | Banco Solidario, S.A. |
| BRI | Bank Rakyat Indonesia |
| CBA | Cost-benefit analysis |
| CEA | Cost-effectiveness analysis |
| CGAP | Consultative Group to Assist the Poorest |
| CNCA | Caisse Nationale de Crédit Agricole |
| EVA | Economic Value Added |
| DFI | Development finance institution |
| GAAP | Generally accepted accounting principles |
| IADB | Inter-American Development Bank |
| IAS | International accounting standard |
| NGO | Nongovernmental organization |
| $NPC_S$ | Net Present Cost to Society |
| PG | Profitability Gap |
| ROA | Return on Assets |
| ROE | Return on Equity |
| SAROA | Subsidy-Adjusted Return on Assets |
| SAROE | Subsidy-Adjusted Return on Equity |
| SDI | Subsidy Dependence Index in a short time frame |
| $SDI_L$ | Subsidy Dependence Index in a long time frame |
| SDR | Subsidy Dependence Ratio |

# Glossary of Notation

| | |
|---|---|
| $c$ | Rate paid for public debt by a DFI |
| $A$ | Average public debt |
| $A \cdot (m - c)$ | Discount on public debt |
| $\delta$ | Social discount rate |
| $d$ | Deposit interest rate |
| $Dep$ | Average deposit liabilities |
| $DG$ | Direct grants |
| $DX$ | Discount on expenses |
| $E$ | Average equity |
| $EG$ | Equity grant |
| $i$ | Yield on loans |
| $I$ | Average investments |
| $j$ | Yield on investments |
| $\kappa$ | Yield received by DFI on required reserves |
| $k$ | Reserve requirement |
| $L$ | Leverage |
| $LP$ | Average loan portfolio (net) |
| $LP \cdot i$ | Revenue from loans |
| $m$ | Opportunity cost of public funds in nominal terms to society or the opportunity cost of public debt to a private entity |
| $M$ | Opportunity cost of public equity to a private entity |
| $n$ | Age of a DFI in years |
| $P$ | Accounting profit |
| $Q$ | Quantity of public funds |
| $\pi$ | Inflation rate |
| $PC$ | Paid-in capital |
| $R$ | Nominal rate of interest |
| $r$ | Real rate of interest |
| $RG$ | Revenue grant |
| $S$ | Subsidy |
| $t$ | Index of years since the start of a time frame |
| $T$ | Years in a time frame |
| $TP$ | True profit |

# Introduction

Why measure the social cost of public development finance institutions? Governments and donors for decades have tried to improve social welfare through public support for development finance institutions (DFIs). Public DFIs, as with all projects that use public funds, are worthwhile in principle only if their social benefits exceed their social costs. In practice, it is so expensive to measure social benefits that a full-blown social cost-benefit analysis (CBA) cannot be done each time a choice must be made to spend public funds on a DFI. A less-expensive alternative to CBA is a simple measure of social cost. *Social cost* is defined as the opportunity cost of public resources used by a DFI. It is the opportunity cost to society of the public funds used by a DFI less what the DFI could pay for those funds and still show a profit. A DFI with no social cost is *subsidy-independent*.

This monograph presents two measures of social cost. The first is the Subsidy Dependence Index (SDI) proposed by Yaron (1992a, 1992b). The second is the Net Present Cost to Society ($NPC_S$) proposed by Schreiner (1997) for the flows of public funds between society and a DFI. The SDI works in short time frames such as a year. Like all other standard present-value measures, the $NPC_S$ works in all time frames because it discounts resource flows according to when they take place in time.

Common financial measures such as accounting profit or Return on Equity (ROE) are based on prices paid as recorded in the accounts of the DFI, and these prices may reflect market failures or nonmarket rules of governments or donors. In contrast, the SDI and the $NPC_S$ are based on *social opportunity costs*, the social return those funds would earn in their best use outside of DFIs. This paradigm shift matters because the prices of public funds entrusted to a DFI as loans or equity are almost always set far below the social opportunity cost. Likewise, DFIs often record grants in cash as revenues and/or fail to record grants in kind as expenses. This practice lards profits but does not change business performance. Such accounting window dressing can hide the truth about the use of public funds by a DFI and its economic subsidy dependence. Generally accepted accounting principles (GAAP) take the opportunity cost of equity as zero and ignore both low levels of inflation and the time value of money. Thus, a DFI can boast of an accounting profit even as inflation shrinks its net worth in real terms. A positive ROE does not always mean that a DFI can compensate society for the opportunity cost of public funds.

The SDI and the $NPC_S$ resolve the problems of accounting-based measures because they value funds at their opportunity costs. They help to check whether a DFI uses public funds to increase or to decrease social welfare. A DFI increases social welfare only if the net benefits from its use of public funds exceed the net benefits from their use elsewhere.

Measurement of the social cost of public support for DFIs matters because public funds are scarce. New measures—such as the SDI and the $NPC_S$—are needed because the old ones fail to measure social costs well because they were designed for private firms, not for public DFIs. The goal of the measurement of social cost is not to end subsidies for DFIs; rather, the goal is to put a price tag on DFIs to make sure that subsidies for DFIs are the best way to improve social welfare.

Appropriate measurements of performance matter because DFIs use a big chunk of the development budget. For example, the World Bank had loaned more than $30 billion (all dollar amounts are U.S. dollars unless specified) for credit projects by 1989 (Von Pischke 1991). Even if donor lending for DFIs dwindles—which seems unlikely given the myriad specialized-credit programs worldwide—the SDI and $NPC_S$ are still useful as measures of the social cost of the explosion of public support for microfinance DFIs during the past decade. Microfinance DFIs outnumber traditional public-sector DFIs; a 1996 survey of more than 200 microfinance DFIs found 13 million loans worth $7 billion and 45 million deposit accounts worth $19 billion (Paxton 1996). Some microfinance advocates hope to attract more than $21.6 billion to extend microfinance to 100 million families in the next 10 years (RESULTS International 1996). It behooves society to check whether the crusade for microfinance siphons funds away from better ways to improve welfare (box I.1; Mosley and Hulme 1998; Buckley 1997; Rogaly 1996).

## What Is the Subsidy Dependence Index?

Yaron (1992a, 1992b) proposed a two-part framework of outreach and sustainability that has become the most common tool to measure the performance of DFIs (e.g., Gonzalez-Vega and others 1997; Khandker 1996; Chaves and Gonzalez-Vega 1996; Christen and others 1995; Benjamin 1994; Yaron 1994; Hossain 1988).

The SDI is a summary measure of sustainability. It is the ratio of subsidy received by a DFI to revenue from loans to the target group and indicates whether a DFI could compensate society for the opportunity

---

## Box I.1.  Social Cost Is the Road Not Taken

The social cost of public resources used in a DFI is the benefit lost because those resources were not used in another project. For example, the social cost as measured by the SDI of the Caisse Nationale de Crédit Agricole (CNCA), a rural development bank in Morocco, was about $85 million a year. According to Devarajan, Squire, and Suthiwart-Narueput (1997, p. 40), these subsidies "could conceivably be justified on the grounds that the bank operated in an underserved rural credit market and reached poor people. Although these benefits are hard to quantify, assessing the cost of the subsidy is one way to ask whether this subsidy is a good use of scarce public resources and to think about alternative uses. In this case, CNCA's annual subsidy amounted to about 20 percent of the recurrent budget for primary education and 160 percent of the recurrent budget for basic health care. And this in a country where social indicators were quite unsatisfactory—primary enrollment is around 70 percent, and under-five mortality is about 80 deaths per thousand live births." Even without a full-blown CBA, the SDI can help to guide the best mix of public investments among, as in this example, agricultural credit, education, and preventative health care.

---

cost of public funds used in a short time frame and still show a profit. Such a DFI is called *subsidy-independent.*

The SDI looks at social cost. The second half of the framework—*outreach*—looks at social benefit. Outreach has six aspects (Schreiner 1999a): worth to users, cost to users, breadth, length, depth, and scope of the output of a DFI.

The SDI relates to subsidy in two ways. First, the SDI provides a framework to measure subsidy as the social opportunity cost of the public funds held by the DFI in a short time frame such as one year, minus the price the DFI paid, minus (plus) accounting profit (loss). Thus, subsidy is the implicit "rental cost" of public resources, minus the rented funds that were lost and thus cannot be returned. Subsidy is positive for a subsidy-dependent DFI and negative for a subsidy-independent DFI.

Second, the SDI is a ratio that uses the measurement of subsidy as its numerator and revenue from loans as its denominator. The ratio can be seen as the percentage change in the yield on loans that, all else constant, would make the DFI subsidy-independent. It may also be seen as the matching grant (subsidy in the numerator) awarded to the DFI by society for each dollar of interest and fees paid by borrowers (revenue from loans in the denominator).

The subsidy measure in the SDI can also be transformed into a Subsidy-Adjusted ROE (SAROE). As will be shown later, the two measures are equivalent in that the SDI is negative if and only if an SAROE would exceed the social opportunity cost. The measure of subsidy in the SDI has features like those of Economic Value Added (EVA), a popular new measure of the financial performance of for-profit firms (box I.2).

---

### Box I.2. Economic Value Added, Subsidy for For-Profit Firms

The concept of the measurement of performance as opportunity cost less profit is not unique to DFIs, having long been a staple in the analysis of not-for-profit hospitals (Jennings 1993; Wheeler and Clement 1990; Silvers and Kauer 1986; Pauly 1986; Conrad 1984, 1986). Nor is the concept unique to not-for-profits. For-profit firms—"lost in ever darker muddles of accounting" (Tully 1993)—have turned to measures based on opportunity cost because measures such as accounting profit and ROE do not tell owners whether a firm increases private wealth, just as they do not tell policymakers whether a DFI increases social welfare.

Subsidy in the SDI is analogous to the concept of Economic Value Added (EVA), a new performance measure used by for-profit firms (*The Economist* 1997). EVA is after-tax profit minus the economic cost of funds used. If EVA is positive, then the firm created financial value for its owners; likewise, if subsidy is negative, then the DFI created financial value for society.

EVA is useful to stockholders because "stock prices track EVA far more closely than they track such popular measures as earnings per share or operating margins or ROE. That is because EVA shows what investors really care about—the net cash return on their capital—rather than some other type of performance viewed through the often distorting lens of accounting rules" (Tully 1993).

Wal-Mart, Coca-Cola, AT&T, and Proctor & Gamble use EVA because, unlike standard accounting measures, EVA accounts for the total cost of capital. One analyst said, "Capital looks free to a lot of managers. It doesn't look free to investors who hand them the money" (Tully 1993). Just as EVA reminds managers of for-profit firms of opportunity costs to investors, the SDI reminds managers of DFIs of opportunity costs to society.

Like the SDI, a strength of EVA is its ease of use. Better measures—such as Net Present Value for stockholders and the Net Present Cost to Society—use discounting, but they are used less because they are more complex.

Measurement with the SDI or EVA boosts performance and ratchets standards up a notch. One CFO said, "The effect is staggering. 'Good' is no longer positive operating earnings. It's only when you beat the cost of capital" (Tully 1993).

Like the SDI, EVA "is powerful and widely applicable because in the end it doesn't prescribe doing anything. . . . Instead, it is a way to see and understand what is really happening" (Tully 1993).

## What Are the Strengths of the Subsidy Dependence Index?

The SDI has at least 12 strengths.

- The SDI quantifies subsidy and shows the extent of subsidy dependence. Often governments and donors do not know just how much their support for DFIs costs society because much of the subsidy is not in terms of explicit cash flows from the public purse to the DFI. Knowledge of subsidies is needed to compare support for DFIs with other uses of public funds.
- The SDI compares subsidy with revenue from loans. This ratio can be seen as a matching grant; that is, the amount of subsidy awarded to the DFI by society for each dollar of interest paid by borrowers.
- The SDI is a measure of subsidy dependence through time. Whether or not a DFI can declare complete subsidy independence, it can always strive to improve.
- A negative SDI implies an SAROE higher than the social opportunity cost. This patches the weaknesses in the common framework based on unadjusted ROE.
- The SDI shifts the paradigm from accounting costs to opportunity costs because accounting costs are often distorted by subsidies.
- The SDI highlights the possibility of covering costs with revenue from loans.
- Although the SDI does not measure benefits, which is expensive, it does measure costs, which is less expensive.
- The SDI is simple—if the financial data of the DFI conform with GAAP—and well known.
- The use of the SDI can induce a disciplined approach to the judgment of the social costs of public support for DFIs.
- Because the data needed for the SDI should be easy to extract, the use of the SDI can highlight specific improvements that should be introduced in the accounting systems.
- The SDI can help in the analysis of the sources and uses of subsidy (Yaron 1992b, p. 24).
- The SDI—unlike the SAROE—worsens if DFIs keep profit constant but shift resources away from loans to the target group and toward other investments such as government bonds.

## What Are the Limitations of the Subsidy Dependence Index?

The SDI has at least two limitations. Analysts should know them so that they use the SDI only to answer the question to which it applies. The SDI answers an important question—whether a DFI could compensate society for the opportunity cost of its funds and still show a profit—but it does not answer all the important questions.

First, the SDI does not discount flows of funds. This is not a difficulty in short time frames (such as one year) with low inflation. But not all time frames are short, and inflation can be high. For example, suppose governments or donors need to choose whether to start a new DFI from scratch. To inform this choice, they might ask whether an existing DFI would have been judged as subsidy-independent from its birth had its eventual performance been known at its birth. Or they might want to plan their support so that projected performance in a long time frame meets a goal (Helms 1997). After all, newborn DFIs, just like all newborn firms, lose money until time and growth spread start-up costs and hone technology. Like private investors who judge firms by their Net Present Value, governments and donors must judge DFIs not only in their first year, not only in the most recent year, and not only in the next year, but rather all through their whole lifetimes. Of course, *pro forma* data may have a wide margin of error, but society should follow the lead of private investors, who find that explicit present-value analysis is useful even if based on data of doubtful quality.

Second, the SDI indicates subsidy independence but not self-sustainability (box I.3). A *subsidy-independent* DFI could pay the social opportunity cost of its funds and still show a profit, and a *self-sustainable* DFI can meet its goals now and in the long term. Subsidy independence may not guarantee self-sustainability. For example, private opportunity costs may exceed social opportunity costs, so a subsidy-independent DFI might not be able to pay market prices for private funds and still show a profit should sources of public funds dry up. Also, for example, a subsidy-independent DFI may fail to meet its goals in the long term if it drifts from its development mission. Of course, the SDI—like all performance measures—indicates subsidy independence in the past and not in the future. Past performance is not a guarantee of future results.

## What Is Net Present Cost to Society?

The $NPC_S$ answers the question: *What benefits did society lose because it entrusted public funds to a DFI rather than to some other project?* Like the SDI, the $NPC_S$ uses the social opportunity cost. Unlike the SDI, the $NPC_S$ discounts flows. Discounting matters more and more as a time frame lengthens.

The $NPC_S$ complements the SDI. To match the practice of the SDI, the $NPC_S$ adds financial flows from society to the DFI and subtracts financial flows from the DFI to society, so the $NPC_S$ is the negative of Net Present Value, a basic yardstick in finance and economics.

---

**Box I.3. Social Worthwhileness, Subsidy Independence, Private Profitability, and Self-Sustainability**

The four concepts of social worthwhileness, subsidy independence, private profitability, and self-sustainability are distinct (Schreiner 1997). A *socially worthwhile* DFI has social benefits that exceed costs in present-value terms. A *subsidy-independent* DFI could pay the social opportunity cost of public funds and still show a profit. A *privately profitable* DFI could pay the private opportunity cost of all funds and still show a profit. A *self-sustainable* DFI could meet its goals now and in the long term.

Social worthwhileness matters because public support for DFIs aims to improve social welfare. Subsidy independence matters because, if customers benefit from a DFI and if there are no external social costs, then zero social cost implies social worthwhileness. Private profitability matters because if public funds are limited then DFIs will be few and small unless private investors use their own funds to buy DFIs or to start new ones from scratch. Finally, self-sustainability matters because society cares about improved welfare both now and in the future.

Subsidy independence is necessary and sufficient for private profitability only if the social opportunity cost equals or exceeds the private opportunity cost. Private profitability is needed, however, for self-sustainability. Privately profitable DFIs may also improve social welfare more than subsidy-dependent DFIs (Schreiner 1999a; Mosley and Hulme 1998; Chaves and Gonzalez-Vega 1996; Rosenberg 1996; Yaron 1994). Privately profitable DFIs may also attract private funds and thus produce more development finance at less cost to the public purse (Rosenberg 1994).

While private profitability is needed for self-sustainability, it does not guarantee it. Self-sustainability also requires a host of other nonfinancial qualities such as organizational strength, efficient technology, a consistent structure of incentives to give stakeholders reasons to act in the interests of the mission of the DFI, and rules that build in flexibility to adjust through time (Schmidt 1997; Schreiner 1995). An investor—whether public or private—that contemplates the purchase of a DFI should check more than just past financial performance because future success depends greatly on intangible, nonfinancial assets.

---

Both Net Present Value and the $NPC_S$ answer the same questions and are derived from standard benefit-cost theory (Gittinger 1982). The two measures have the same magnitude and opposite signs. If customers get more benefits than costs and if noncustomers do not bear any costs, then a DFI started from scratch that is equivalent to a DFI with a negative $NPC_S$ would be expected to be a good social investment. Likewise, a DFI with a negative $NPC_S$ seen from now on is a good social investment from now on.

Wise use of the $NPC_S$ recognizes three facts. First, the $NPC_S$ is not just the sum of SDIs through a span of years. Second, a negative $NPC_S$ as seen from now on does not necessarily imply a negative $NPC_S$ as seen from birth. Because past costs are sunk, public support for a DFI from now on may make sense even though it would not have made sense had future performance been known at the time of birth. Third, the $NPC_S$ ignores benefits and costs to noncustomers. If these benefits exceed these costs, then a DFI with a positive $NPC_S$ (or a positive SDI) could still be a good use of public funds.

## Is the Subsidy Dependence Index Redundant?

Unlike the SDI, the $NPC_S$ discounts flows. Thus, the $NPC_S$ measures social cost better than the SDI, especially in long time frames or when the social rate of time preference is high. All else constant, society would be better off if it judged DFIs not only with the SDI but also with the $NPC_S$, especially in long time frames. Still, the SDI is far from redundant for three reasons. First, the SDI is slightly easier to compute than the one-year case of the $NPC_S$. Second, the extra accuracy caused by discounting in the one-year case of the $NPC_S$ may be dwarfed by the inaccuracies of the basic data and by the coarse assumptions used by both the SDI and the $NPC_S$ in the attempt to fit data based on GAAP accounting into a economic framework. Third and most important, many people already are familiar with ROE, so the SDI is useful in its guise as a Subsidy-Adjusted ROE.

Because the $NPC_S$ discounts cash flows and the SDI does not, the two measures do not answer the same question. Society might ask about social cost (or the Subsidy-Adjusted ROE) of a DFI in a short time frame, and the answer is contained in the SDI. Society might also ask about social cost in long time frames, and the answer is the $NPC_S$. Both questions and answers matter, and both the SDI and the $NPC_S$ are the right tools for their own distinct purposes.

Neither the SDI nor the $NPC_S$ answers all questions about the performance of a DFI. The two measures inform some questions, but they do not inform all questions, nor do they fully inform any single question. Like all financial ratios, the SDI and the $NPC_S$ do not tell directly why performance is good or bad, nor do they tell directly how to improve. Other quantitative indicators and qualitative analysis still have a role in the full assessment of the performance of public DFIs. In particular, further analysis and even full-blown benefit-cost analysis might be desirable in some circumstances despite its high cost.

## What Does the Rest of the Monograph Cover?

Chapter 1 discusses why DFIs exist and why society would want to measure their performance.

Chapter 2 presents the formula of the SDI in terms of the basic accounts of a set of financial statements for an example DFI. It also has numerical examples and discusses what the SDI means and shows how the measure of subsidy in the SDI can also be transformed into a Subsidy-Adjusted ROE.

Chapter 3 derives the $NPC_S$ and gives numerical examples. It also shows that the one-year case of the $NPC_S$ is not the same as the SDI.

Chapter 4 emphasizes that the SDI and the $NPC_S$ are only as good as their data and assumptions. It notes pitfalls in their calculation, especially the need to adjust financial statements to reflect the repayment risk of outstanding loans and to purge the effects of inflation.

Chapter 5 reviews three recent attempts to modify the SDI or to use other standards to judge the performance of public DFIs. It makes explicit the questions answered by these new proposals and argues that their use does not lead to a better understanding of the social cost of public DFIs.

# 1

# Why Measure the Social Cost of Public Development Finance Institutions?

The measurement of the social cost of public DFIs matters because public funds budgeted for development are scarce. The poor can use loans and deposits, but they can also use more and/or better food, water, air, health, clothes, houses, schools, roads, fuels, skills, tools, laws, markets, and/or safety. The SDI and the $NPC_S$ are two measures of social cost. Neither the SDI nor the $NPC_S$ is equivalent to social CBA, but both measures are linked to self-sustainability and to social welfare.

Oversight of public DFIs is needed because the people who work for governments and donors and who choose to support DFIs with public funds do not bear most of the costs and benefits of that choice. Instead, costs and benefits accrue to taxpayers (because they provide public funds), customers of the DFI (from the use of services), and noncustomers (from displacement by customers and from the loss of benefits from projects left unfunded). Oversight is also needed because DFIs tempt governments and donors more than most development projects because they involve self-help not with gifts but with loans (Mosley and Hulme 1998). Measurement of the social cost of public DFIs aims to help to align private incentives with the public good.

## What Is a Public Development Finance Institution?

A public DFI is a financial intermediary that aims to improve social welfare and that gets some resources from governments or donors. A public DFI may be owned by the state and thus receive public resources as equity, but it may also have private owners (or no owners) and receive public resources as gifts or loans. Public funds entrusted to a DFI are subsidized because the unfettered market would charge more. If not, then the DFI would refuse public funds and go straight to the market on its own. By the same logic, a DFI subsidizes its clients. If services from a public DFI were costlier than identical services from the market, then clients would eschew the DFI.

## Who Bears the Costs and Who Reaps the Benefits of Public Development Finance Institutions?

Society—all the people in the world or all the people in a country—bears the cost of public DFIs. Subsidies to one person are taxes to another. Furthermore, funds spent on a DFI are funds not spent to improve welfare in some other way. The direct or primary benefits of a public DFI accrue to its clients. Although indirect or secondary costs and benefits to nonclients and to the employees of the DFI, governments, and donors may be large, they are also very difficult to measure, so this monograph ignores them.

If there are no externalities, then there is no need to measure social costs and benefits when private people transfer their own funds to a DFI. It is safe to assume that private people look out for their own good and thus weigh benefits and costs as they see them. In contrast, there is a need to measure social costs and benefits when governments and donors transfer funds to DFIs. Public servants do not always look out for the public good (Stiglitz 1998; Tollison 1984). Analysis is warranted because the group that bears the costs is not the group that gets the benefits (Brent 1996).

Worse, the choice to subsidize DFIs may be in the hands of the very same employees who stand to gain from the subsidies because more funds for DFIs maintain their jobs, foster promotion, and expand their influence. This group is small, organized, and vocal. Each member may have a lot to gain from channeling more subsidies to DFIs. Furthermore, the subsidies linked to loans from DFIs may attract rich people. If loans are big so that subsidies are big, then rich people may find it worthwhile to press for more public funds for DFIs. For example, rich farmers and their lobbies sought and received big subsidies from agricultural DFIs all over the world (Adams, Graham, and Von Pischke 1984).

In contrast, the groups who bear the brunt of the costs of public DFIs are taxpayers and nonclients left unhelped by projects left unfunded. These groups are big, dispersed, and silent. The small cost to each member of the group means that it is not worth their effort to press for cuts in public support for DFIs.

Because changes in personal welfare caused by public support for DFIs are not perfectly aligned with changes in social welfare, industry lobbies and employees of governments, donors, and DFIs may be tempted to crusade for DFIs even if DFIs are not the best way to improve social welfare. Alternatively, policymakers may lack the tools or the data to check whether a DFI improves social welfare. The decision makers must be watched because they may get benefits without bearing the costs. The measurement of costs can help to remind them of the worth of public funds in DFIs versus in alternative uses.

## How Do Public Development Finance Institutions Differ from Other Public Projects?

Public DFIs resemble most other projects that get public funds. The people who bear the costs are not the same people who get the benefits, and there are small groups whose jobs and rents depend on more funds. DFIs also hold an uncommonly tempting promise of development potential because they work with financial capital, a factor often seen as a constraint on development. DFIs transfer control over assets, and the poor are poor because they lack the assets that produce income (Sherraden 1991). DFIs are also politically correct. They do not give money away; rather, they lend it at interest. Few dare oppose helping others help themselves.

DFIs differ from other public development projects in their unusual susceptibility to abuse. The benefits of DFIs for clients are easy to see, but costs are often obscure. No one can argue with the worth of a loan that helps an orphan married at 12 and abandoned at 13 to buy land and to send her child to school (RESULTS International 1996). In contrast, even skilled financial analysts often overlook the opportunity costs of a public DFI or the erosion of the real value of its equity. Measures of cost can help decision makers to remember not only the faces of a few recipients but also the faceless millions who do not get projects because funds go to DFIs. The choice is not between a public DFI or nothing at all; rather, the choice is between a public DFI or some other project to improve welfare.

DFIs are also susceptible to abuse because, on the surface, making loans requires only money. Compared with other development projects, DFIs are easy to start and to run because anyone with money—regardless of technical expertise—can make loans (Ladman and Tinnermeier 1981).

DFIs may also attract—from a social point of view—too much donor funds because they can absorb and disburse funds fast. It can be easier to lend than to spend, especially if repayment is not a concern (Von Pischke 1991). Public support for DFIs may also offer politicians a convenient way to hide transfers of wealth (Ladman and Tinnermeier 1981). To sum up, the potential for the abuse of a DFI is high.

## Why Does Society Subsidize Public Development Finance Institutions?

Society subsidizes DFIs to improve social welfare (Yaron, Benjamin, and Piprek 1997). The social benefit is the extra utility of clients with the DFI versus without it. The social cost is the benefit lost because the DFI was funded instead of something else.

In principle, a market failure is required for public DFIs to improve social welfare. A *market failure* is when competition fails to lead to a socially efficient outcome (Besley 1994). This happens when a movement from the status quo would improve social welfare, but no private entity can capture enough of the gains to recoup its costs. The market fails because the best private choice is not also the best social choice. In principle, someone could be made better off and no one would be worse off.

In practice, market failures plague financial markets (Stiglitz 1993). But market failure, though needed to justify public intervention, is not enough. DFIs can be justified only if they mitigate a market failure so well that the benefits due to the intervention exceed the costs due to the intervention. Even in the absence of market failure, a public DFI might be the best way to reach a social goal, for example, if no other tool addresses an important social concern as efficiently (Yaron, Benjamin, and Piprek 1997).

DFIs venture where the market failed, and to find good borrowers shunned by private lenders is a difficult task. Through adjustments to the ways in which they judge and control risk, some DFIs have found profitable ways to make loans and to get repaid without traditional collateral. Often, the most successful DFIs are those most concerned about the measurement of their costs.

In the past, DFIs have often backfired, and they may even have hurt those they meant to help (Yaron, Benjamin, and Piprek 1997; Hulme and Mosley 1996; Krahnen and Schmidt 1994; Adams, Graham, and Von Pischke 1984). "In practice, DFIs found it difficult to finance projects with high economic but low financial rates of return and to remain financially viable at the same time" (World Bank 1989, p. 106). Subsidies grew, strained budgets, and failed to strengthen the DFIs so that they could survive without subsidies. For example, Mexico put more than $23 billion in 1992 dollars in agricultural DFIs from 1983 to 1992 before budget cuts forced a decrease (World Bank 1994).

Of course, some DFIs are good and do mitigate market failures. But some other DFIs may waste scarce funds or exacerbate market failures. The theory is clear; if there is a market failure, then a DFI might have scope to improve social welfare. In practice, however, market failure alone is not enough to justify a DFI because DFIs themselves have costs and can disrupt markets. Government failure may wreck attempts to fix market failure, or a DFI might be inefficient. To choose well, society must measure costs, and perhaps also benefits (Devarajan, Squire, and Suthiwart-Narueput 1997).

A DFI is only one of a number of possibly complementary ways to improve welfare through reduced poverty and increased incomes.

According to Lipton and Ravaillon (1995, p. 2630), "Chronic poverty does not appear to be due mainly to 'market failure' in credit or other markets, but rather to low factor productivity and low endowments-per-person of nonlabor factors."

## How Can Society Measure the Benefits of Public Development Finance Institutions?

The benefits of DFIs are the extra welfare of clients with a DFI versus without. The comparison is not before-and-after but rather with-and-without. A before-and-after comparison does not control for the changes in welfare that would have happened regardless of access to the DFI (Gittinger 1982). The problem is to know what would have happened without the DFI, the standard counter-factual problem. This requires a control group: people who cannot choose to use the DFI but who are just like the people who can choose to use it in all ways. Getting a control group usually requires random assignment of access to a DFI (or random assignment of qualified applicants), but such social experiments consume large amounts of funds, time, and expertise and are still subject to potentially debilitating critiques (Heckman and Smith 1995). The only social experiment with random assignment ever in development finance tests the effects of access to Individual Development Accounts and is currently taking place in Tulsa, Oklahoma (Schreiner 2000a; Sherraden and others 2000).

Without a control group, there is no inexpensive way to measure the impact of a DFI. For example, a dollar from a DFI is the same as a dollar from any other source. This fungibility of money means that, without a control group, the analyst cannot know if the loan caused an observed outcome or if the outcome would have happened anyway (Adams 1988; Adams and Von Pischke 1992; David and Meyer 1983; Von Pischke and Adams 1980). Once the difficulties caused by fungibility became clear and widely accepted, serious work to measure the benefits of DFIs went dormant.

While fungibility does indeed wreck before-and-after comparisons, it does not affect with-and-without comparisons between randomly assigned treatment and control groups because random assignment controls for all other factors that might affect outcomes. While good measurements cost a lot and while wrong measurements could be worse than no measurements, it does not follow that no one should try to make good measurements.

In the absence of random assignment, the measurement of the benefits of a DFI is similar to program evaluation with nonexperimental data. Econometricians have grappled with this problem for at least 30 years

(Moffitt 1991). Their research has concluded that the analyst must control for the systematic differences—whether observed or unobserved—between clients and nonclients. Rigorous attempts to do this for DFIs include, among others, Montgomery, Johnson, and Faisal (2000); Amin, Rai, and Topa (1999); Coleman (1999); McKnelly and Dunford (1998); Morduch (1998); Mosley and Hulme (1998); Pitt and Khandker (1998); Smith and Jain (1998); Carter and Olinto (1996); McKernan (1996); Sial and Carter (1996); Lapar (1995); Bolnick and Nelson (1990); Feder and others (1990); and Carter (1989).

Without random assignment, a good control group is hard to find. Among the people who have access to a DFI, the people who choose to use the DFI are not the same as the people who choose not to use the DFI; the users are more likely to do well regardless of the DFI, perhaps because they work more or accept higher risks. In contrast, the nonusers likely would not do so well regardless of the DFI. Thus, simple comparisons of users to nonusers may overestimate the impact of the DFI.

Although the measurement of benefits is improving all the time, credible measures are still incomplete and require a long time, a lot of skill, and a big budget. Thus, it is too expensive to measure the benefits of all public DFIs (Yaron, Benjamin, and Piprek 1997). Also, while a study may estimate the impact of a DFI on one outcome, it is much more difficult to estimate the impact of a DFI on all outcomes of interest.

In contrast, it is less expensive to measure costs. In most cases, the measurement of costs but not benefits is a better use of resources than the measurement of both costs and benefits. This is the basic premise behind cost-effectiveness analysis (CEA) (Garber and Phelps 1997; Weinstein and Stason 1977). Whereas CBA compares costs with expensive-to-measure benefits, CEA compares costs with inexpensive-to-measure outputs. Of course, CEA is not as useful as full-blown CBA. For example, CEA cannot rank projects that do not produce the same outputs for the same customers. Also, CEA cannot tell whether benefits exceed costs. Examples of CEA for development finance are Morduch (1999), Schreiner (1997), Binswanger and Khandker (1995), and Gale (1991). CEA is the essence of the measurement of the cost of public provision, suggested by Devarajan, Squire, and Suthiwart-Narueput (1997) as one of two keys for better project appraisal.

Of course, the fact that the measurement of costs is less expensive than the measurement of benefits does not mean that only costs matter to the exclusion of benefits. It just means that in discussions of the social worth of DFIs, analysts will often be able to be more explicit about costs than about benefits. Choices about what public projects to fund ultimately must rely on informed judgments of both costs and benefits, even if knowledge of costs is better than knowledge of benefits.

# What Is the Opportunity Cost to Society of Public Funds Used by Development Finance Institutions?

The social cost of a public DFI is the return its public funds could get in their best other use. This return is called the *opportunity cost*, the *efficiency price*, or the *shadow price*. A dollar used on one thing cannot be used on something else.

The most important parameter in the measurement of the social cost of public DFIs is the opportunity cost to society of public funds. The choice of an appropriate opportunity cost will often drive the main results of the analysis. This parameter is so expensive to measure that the analyst must choose a proxy or simply make an assumption. While there are no foolproof rules, this section provides some criteria and guidelines for the choice.

## Are Social and Private Opportunity Costs the Same?

Social and private opportunity costs are not the same. For both society and for private entities, the opportunity cost is the return that funds could earn in a use of similar risk. But social and private opportunity costs may diverge for two reasons. First, public and private investors do not in general have the same opportunities, budgets, or constraints. For example, public funds earmarked for development must be spent on development projects. Private investors have no such constraint.

Second, private and social costs and benefits may diverge due to market failures caused by externalities, public goods, transaction costs, principal-agent problems, and/or information asymmetries. Private investors count only their own costs and benefits. As a result, they may ignore some projects with low private returns but high social returns. In contrast, public entities should count all costs and benefits to all people in society. Of course, the existence of market failure does not necessarily justify public intervention (Besley 1994).

In general, the social opportunity cost is at least as high as the private opportunity cost, because society accounts for benefits to all people while private people only account for their own benefits. Furthermore, if a private project has higher returns than a public one, then society can always invest in it as if it were a private owner (Jennings 1993).

## Are Social or Private Opportunity Costs the Same as the Price Paid by a Development Finance Institution for Public Funds?

Neither social nor private opportunity costs are necessarily equal to the price paid by a DFI for public funds. The prices of public funds are set most often not by market feedback but by administrative fiat. For example, one multi-lateral donor has made loans to DFIs with grace periods of 5 years, terms of 40 years, and interest rates of 1 percent. The price of this public debt did not depend on its social opportunity cost, on the expected risk of the DFI, or on the rates and terms of a like loan in the market. Because the price of public funds does not reflect opportunity costs, measures such as accounting profit and ROE do not reflect the performance of a public DFI from a social nor private point of view.

## Do Public Funds as Equity Have the Same Opportunity Cost as Public Funds as Debt?

Public funds labeled as equity in a DFI do not necessarily have the same opportunity cost as public funds labeled as debt because equity does not have a fixed repayment obligation. In general, equity is riskier than debt, so the opportunity cost of equity exceeds that of debt. The appendix reviews a simple method developed by Benjamin (1994) to approximate the private opportunity costs of debt and equity.

For society, debt and equity are the same for DFIs that are completely state-owned or that have explicit or implicit state guarantees for all of their debt. The examples here assume that the DFI is completely state-owned, although most microfinance DFIs are not state-owned and do not enjoy state guarantees on their debt.

If a DFI can take deposits, then it might replace public debt with deposits instead of with private debt. In this case, the private opportunity cost of public debt would be the interest rate paid on deposits plus a markup for the expected increases in the cost of administration and reserve requirements. Still, loans from banks would often replace public debt. In general, deposits will cost more and the DFI will be more likely to use debt rather than deposits as the DFI is newer and smaller, has less experience with deposits, is seen as risky by potential depositors, has more debt compared with equity, has more competition, and has more public funds to replace. Many DFIs—and certainly most microfinance DFIs—cannot replace public funds with private deposits because they are not licensed to take deposits.

## What Are Proxies for the Social Opportunity Cost of Public Funds?

In practice, it is so expensive to measure the social opportunity cost of public funds that less-expensive proxies are used. In some cases, governments or donors will have estimates of the return to some unfunded project. But because project analysis itself is costly and is subject to diminishing returns, returns for all funded and unfunded projects will not be known. Furthermore, in practice, some projects are funded for reasons other than their high net social benefits. If governments, donors, and their employees are risk averse, then safe but low-return projects may get funded before risky but high-return projects. With a budget constraint, the best projects should be chosen until funds run out.

The goal of the choice of a social opportunity cost is to measure costs well so as to help to spend public funds better. The choice has four criteria. First, the number should be meaningful, that is, credibly close to the true opportunity cost. Second, all public-sector analyses should use the same opportunity cost because all public projects compete for public funds and because comparisons across projects require the use of a uniform opportunity cost. Third, higher rates are preferred to lower rates, all else constant. This protects society from those who would use low rates to give a false sense of rigor to support their pet projects. Fourth, the rate chosen must be credible. Disagreements about the social opportunity cost sidetrack project analyses more than any other issue.

Figure 1.1 illustrates five possible proxies of the social opportunity cost. The horizontal axis is the amount of funds $Q$. The vertical axis is the nominal social opportunity cost $m$. As the amount $Q$ increases, the mar-

## Figure 1.1. Five Possible Proxies of the Social Opportunity Cost

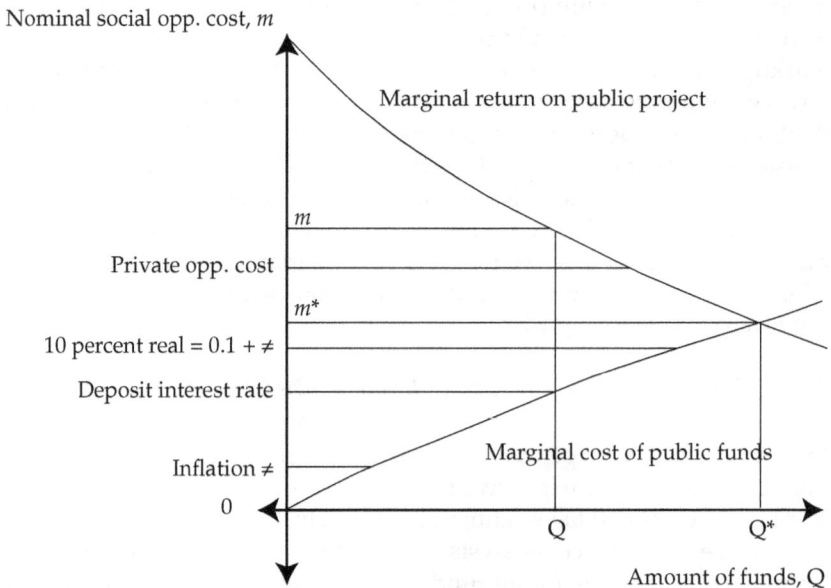

ginal cost of public funds $m$ increases, and the marginal return on public projects decreases. Except for the signs of their slopes, the curves are drawn arbitrarily and are assumed to include all factors that matter for social costs and benefits, for example, the monopoly of the government in the sale of riskless bonds due to its monopoly on the creation of legal tender.

ZERO. Analyses that ignore opportunity costs implicitly assume a zero nominal social opportunity cost. With positive inflation, this implies a negative real social opportunity cost because real rates $r$ are linked to inflation $\pi$ and to nominal rates $R$ through $r \doteq (R - \pi)/(1 + \pi)$. Negative opportunity costs are not credible because the net benefits of the marginal project are positive.

THE RATE OF INFLATION. A second possible proxy for the nominal social opportunity cost is inflation $\pi$. Given positive inflation, then the real social opportunity cost is zero. This is too low (Mishan 1988; Dasgupta and Pearce 1978), in part because it implies that benefits in the present are not preferred to benefits in the future. Some frameworks, however, do use inflation as the nominal social opportunity cost (Rosenberg, Christen, and Helms 1997; Holtmann and Mommartz 1996).

THE RATE OF INTEREST ON DEPOSITS. A third possible proxy is the interest rate for treasury bills or, equivalently, the rate paid for time deposits by state-owned DFIs plus a markup for the expected cost of administration and reserve requirements, commonly assumed to be about two to three percentage points but adjustable to the specific case (Yaron 1992b). Most examples of the SDI use the deposit rate (e.g., Sacay, Randhawa, and Agabin 1996; Khandker, Khalily, and Khan 1995; Yaron 1994). This assumes that the social benefit of the marginal public project equals the marginal cost of funds to the state.

If public funds were raised and spent to the point where marginal cost equals marginal benefit ($Q^*, m^*$ in figure 1.1) and if all other markets were perfectly competitive, frictionless, and without information or transaction costs, then the deposit interest rate would equal both social and private opportunity costs. In this equilibrium case, the social opportunity cost is also a market rate, hence the symbol $m$.

In practice, all markets are not perfect. Instead, governments and donors have limited budgets and more potentially high-return projects than they can fund. In this disequilibrium, the cost of funds raised and spent at $Q$ is not the same as the return on the marginal project $m$. The deposit rate is often less than the social opportunity cost. Thus, measures of subsidy that use the deposit rate are lower bounds (Yaron 1992b).

TEN PERCENT IN REAL TERMS. A fourth possible proxy for the social opportunity cost is 10 percent per year in real terms. This somewhat arbitrary
rate is used by most governments and by the World Bank as a uniform
rule of thumb (Belli 1996a; Katz and Welch 1993; Gittinger 1982). Like all
of the proxies described here, it may be adjusted for risk, although that is
not the best way to analyze risk (Norgaard and Howarth 1992;
Markandya and Pearce 1991).

If the real rate is $r$, then the nominal rate is $r + \pi + r \cdot \pi$. Thus, the nominal rate could be above or below the equilibrium rate $m^*$ in figure 1.1.
Usually, funds will run out before projects with returns above 10 percent.

Although no one claims that 10 percent is particularly close to the true
real rate of return on the marginal public investment, the rate has been
favored in practice for at least three reasons. First, the true return on the
marginal public investment is unknown, and guesses as to its value
inevitably lead to endless debates. Second, compared with the known
rates already discussed, 10 percent is a higher lower bound on the true
marginal social return. Quirk and Terasawa (1991) find that the marginal
return to public investment is probably much higher than 10 percent, and
the estimates of Ballard, Shoven, and Whalley (1985) imply a minimum
social opportunity cost of 17 percent. Third, 10 percent is the number
most widely used. This not only defuses quibbles about its use, but it also
allows cost comparisons across projects. This view treats opportunity
costs less as marginal returns and more as tools to allocate scarce funds
from a budget (Belli 1996a).

Ten percent per year in real terms is a lower bound for the social
opportunity cost. According to Belli (1996a, p. 148), "A discount rate
lower than 10 percent might be difficult to justify." In particular, Gittinger
(1982, p. 315) says that "financial rates of interest, such as government
borrowing rates or the prime lending rate, are generally too low to justify their use in economic [from the point of view of society] analysis of
projects. Indeed, when inflation is high, these rates may even be negative
in real terms." The burden of proof for another opportunity cost rests on
the analyst (Gittinger 1982). The examples in this monograph use 10 percent because it is the highest credible lower bound and because it helps
to make analyses comparable across projects and countries.

THE OPPORTUNITY COST OF FUNDS TO PRIVATE ENTITIES. A fifth possible
proxy for the social opportunity cost is the opportunity cost of private
entities. This is the risk-adjusted price to replace public funds with similar funds from private sources. For example, the private opportunity cost
of equity is the return required to attract and to retain private investors in
the long term. Likewise, the private opportunity cost of public debt is
what a DFI would pay for similar debt from private lenders. Of course,

private opportunity costs vary through time and among DFIs due to differences in risk, leverage, and the local cost of funds. The market price of funds in figure 1.1 is drawn below the marginal return on public projects because the state can always invest in private projects, should private projects have a higher return than public projects (Conrad 1984, 1986; Jennings 1993; Silvers and Kauer 1986).

## Why Does the Measurement of Costs Boost Performance?

The measurement of costs sparks strong performance, casts light on bad performance, and helps to reward good stewards in five ways (Schreiner 1997).

- Measurement forces DFIs and their sponsors to discuss their goals. Foggy goals wither under attempts at measurement. Buzzwords lose punch unless grounded in the nuts-and-bolts problems of measurement (IADB 1994).
- Measurement changes goals. Those who measure costs worry about costs and vice versa (Von Pischke 1996).
- Measurement highlights goals. A DFI that measures costs signals a willingness to reduce costs. Success is more than only disbursement. If donors measure only disbursements, then a DFI will learn to disburse at any cost (Von Pischke 1998).
- Measurement helps to meet goals. Technical feedback helps managers detect trends, set targets, benchmark progress, and compare to peers (Richardson 1994; Koch 1992; Barltrop and McNaughton 1992).
- Measurement proves what is possible for DFIs. Governments and donors want to demand better performance. But without measurement, they are pestered by the fear that they ask for too much too fast. Unsure donors expect less, and they get less (Schmidt and Zeitinger 1996).

# 2
# What Is a Measure of the Social Cost of a Public Development Finance Institution in the Short Term?

A measure of the social cost of a public DFI in the short term is the SDI (Yaron 1992b). The SDI is the dollar value of subsidy divided by revenue from interest and fees on loans. It answers the question: *How far is the DFI from being able to compensate society for the opportunity cost of its funds and still show a profit?* If a DFI could compensate for subsidy, then it is subsidy-independent. Its SDI would be less than zero, and its Subsidy-Adjusted ROE would exceed the social opportunity cost.

The SDI measures the cost of a public DFI and compares it with its activity level. The SDI is a simple tool that shifts the paradigm from reported (accounting) costs to opportunity (economic) costs. Accounting profit and ROE often disguise the performance of public DFIs because some expenses do not reflect social opportunity costs.

The SDI helps to measure progress toward "the phasing out of credit subsidies, the assumption by the fiscal budget of funding responsibility for any remaining subsidies, and the reduction and/or rationalization of directed credit lines" as required by "World Bank Policies Guiding Financial Sector Operations" (paragraph 17). The SDI can help link current public support to progress toward future independence from public support (Women's World Banking 1995).

## How Does a Development Finance Institution Get Subsidies?

A DFI gets subsidies from subsidized funds. *Subsidized funds* are public funds. If a DFI accepts public funds, then it must be that they cost less than private funds. *Subsidy* is the social opportunity cost minus the price the DFI actually pays.

By definition, only public funds can be subsidized, and private funds, regardless of their price, are not subsidized, unless a contribution is tax-exempt or unless the market price is affected by an explicit or implicit state

guarantee of the liabilities of a DFI. The distinction is particularly important for microfinance DFIs that receive some private donations. Unlike
public donors, private donors spend their own money. The fact that the
owner of the funds agrees to entrust them to a DFI reveals that the benefits
of the transaction exceed the costs, at least from the point of view of the private donor. For example, shares in a credit union held by members of their
own free will are not subsidized even if the credit union never pays dividends or buys the shares back. The members choose to buy shares because
they judge that the benefits of membership are worth it. Likewise, compensating balances that pay low rates are not subsidized. The lost earnings
are part of the price borrowers accept when they choose to borrow. Even
outright gifts are not subsidized, as long as they are private. The fact that
private funds are not subsidized does not necessarily mean that the DFI is
efficient, nor that it is privately profitable. It may still be useful to compute
private costs and/or benefits with common measures such as ROE or EVA
(box I.2) that take the private point of view. But no public analysis is needed. Still, the measurement of social cost for DFIs with some public funds
must be careful to exclude funds from private sources.

## What Forms of Subsidized Funds
## Does a Development Finance Institution Get?

Subsidized funds come in six forms (table 2.1). Three forms are equity
grants. Equity grants increase net worth directly but do not directly
change accounting profit reported in the year received. The other three
forms are profit grants. Profit grants increase accounting profit directly
because they inflate revenues and/or deflate expenses. This increases net
worth at year-end indirectly through retained earnings.

Compared with the case without the grant, all six forms increase net
worth one-for-one and have a social opportunity cost equal to $m$. As in
Yaron (1992b), this monograph ignores dividends and taxes on profits in
the interest of simplicity.

### Table 2.1. Types of Subsidized Funds

| Type of subsidized funds | Notation | Type of grant |
| --- | --- | --- |
| Direct grant | DG | Equity grant (EG) |
| Paid-in capital | PC | Equity grant (EG) |
| Revenue grant | RG | Profit grant (PG) |
| Discount on public debt | $A \cdot (m - c)$ | Profit grant (PG) |
| Discount on expenses | DX | Profit grant (PG) |
| True profit | TP | Equity grant (EG) |

Source: Authors.

## Equity Grants

The first two forms of subsidized funds are equity grants $EG$. These cash gifts increase net worth but do not change the accounting profit reported in a period directly. Equity grants are the sum of direct grants $DG$ and paid-in capital $PC$:

$$\text{equity grants} = \text{direct grants} + \text{paid-in capital}$$
$$EG = DG + PC. \tag{2.1}$$

Direct grants $DG$ are cash gifts. Direct grants increase net worth, but they do not pass through the income statement, and so they do not inflate accounting profit. Direct grants include both gifts in cash and gifts in kind such as computers or trucks.

Paid-in capital $PC$ comes from sales of shares to governments or donors. Such a sale is like a direct grant because public funds pay for the shares. Furthermore, most donors do not wield control like private owners. This monograph assumes that all paid-in capital comes from public sources.

## Profit Grants

Profit grants are the third through fifth forms of subsidized funds (table 2.1). Like all equity grants, all forms of profit grants $PG$ increase net worth because they inflate accounting profit or reduce accounting loss and thus increase retained earnings.

Profit grants are the sum of revenue grants $RG$, discounts on public debt $A \cdot (m - c)$, and discounts on expenses $DX$:

$$\text{profit grants} = \text{revenue grants} + \text{discount on public debt}$$
$$+ \text{discount on expenses} \tag{2.2}$$
$$PG = RG + A \cdot (m - c) + DX.$$

Profit grants distort accounting profit $P$ and thus ROE because they depend not on business performance but on arbitrary choices by administrators and accountants. Donors can use profit grants to nudge accounting profit and ROE as high or as low as they like. In contrast to accounting profit and ROE, the SDI and the $NPC_S$ recognize that a dollar treated as a profit grant has the same effect on business performance as a dollar treated as an equity grant (box 2.1; figure 2.1).

Revenue grants $RG$ are cash gifts. They are just like equity grants except for the accounting choice to record them as revenue instead of as direct injections to equity. Revenue grants increase net worth, but only

## Box 2.1. How Profit Grants Affect Profit and Return on Equity

Governments and donors can give a DFI a dollar through equity grants or profit grants. The choice affects nothing of substance because all grants increase equity one-for-one and have the same opportunity cost. Unlike equity grants, however, profit grants boost accounting profit and thus ROE. Profit grants are equity injections, but they enter the accounts as if they were operating revenue. Classifying a dollar as a profit grant instead of as an equity grant increases accounting profit but does not change business performance.

For example, suppose a donor injects $100 in a DFI at a smooth pace through a year. The DFI starts with equity of $100. In the first case, the donor gives all $100 as equity grants and none as profit grants. Equity grants do not affect revenues or expenses, and the DFI posts an accounting loss of $50. End equity is the sum of start equity, equity grants, and profit, so average equity is $(100 + 100 + 100 - 50)/2 = 125$. ROE is $-50/125 = -0.40$. In this first case, ROE correctly states that the DFI destroyed 40 cents for each dollar of equity used (see figure 2.1).

Now suppose all $100 shifts from equity grants to profit grants. Revenues increase and/or expenses decrease, so now profit is $50 even though business performance is unchanged. Average equity is still 125, but ROE is now $50/125 = 0.40$. In this second case, ROE incorrectly states that the DFI created 40 cents for each dollar of equity used (see figure 2.1).

Accounting profit and ROE depend on the arbitrary choice to record subsidized funds as equity grants or profit grants. These measures may hide the true performance of a DFI because they depend on the arbitrary form of subsidized funds. Many DFIs do not adhere to GAAP and thus may record grants or reimbursements of expenses not as equity injections but as revenue.

### Figure 2.1. Profit Grants and ROE

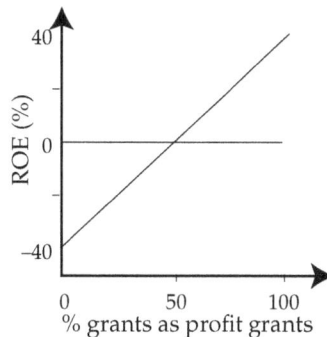

The distinction matters for meaningful measures of financial performance.

Other common financial ratios have the same weaknesses. In contrast, the SDI and the $NPC_S$ do not change as profit grants change. Christen (1997) also proposes an elegant approach that adjusts the financial statements themselves so that common ratios answer the questions they are meant to answer for public DFIs.

after they pass through the income statement and inflate accounting profit. Because revenue grants are not the product of the business operations of the DFI, they should not be in reported profit.

Discounts on public debt $A \cdot (m - c)$ and discounts on expenses $DX$ are the fourth and fifth forms of subsidized funds. They are noncash gifts, expenses paid on behalf of the DFI by someone else. Discounts increase the profit reported by the DFI because they decrease expenses.

The discount on public debt $A \cdot (m - c)$ is the opportunity cost of public debt less what the DFI paid, where $A$ is average public debt, $c$ is the rate the DFI paid for public debt, and $m$ is the social opportunity cost of public debt:

$$\begin{aligned} \text{discount public debt} &= \text{average public debt} \\ &\quad \cdot (\text{opportunity cost public debt} - \text{rate paid}) \quad (2.3) \\ &= A \cdot (m \cdot c). \end{aligned}$$

Like all discounts, discounts on public debt are subsidized funds that inflate profit and boost net worth because they cut expenses. Public debt is like private debt linked to a grant of $A \cdot (m - c)$ (IADB 1994). Unlike the *discount* on public debt, *public debt* itself does not increase net worth.

The average rate paid on public debt $c$ is the expense for interest paid on public debt, divided by the average public debt $A$:

$$c = \frac{\text{expense for interest for public debt}}{\text{average public debt}}. \qquad (2.4)$$

The best way to estimate average public debt $A$ is to track the dates and the amounts of each inflow and outflow and then to find the average daily balance. Usually, such detailed data are unavailable to external analysts. A common practice is to estimate $A$ as half the sum of the public debt at the start of the year $A_0$ and at the end of the year $A_1$, although quarterly or monthly averages would be more accurate:

$$A = (A_0 + A_1)/2. \qquad (2.5)$$

Discounts on expenses $DX$ are costs absorbed by governments or donors that the DFI does not record as expenses. Classic examples are technical help, free deposit insurance, coverage of organization costs or feasibility studies, debt guarantees, fees for consultants, classes for loan officers, and travel for employees. Although discounts on expenses often leave no trace in the financial statements and are difficult to track, they are common and may represent large resource transfers (Schreiner 2000b).

## True Profit

True profit *TP*, the sixth form of subsidized funds (table 2.1), is like an equity grant. True profit is accounting profit *P* less profit grants (equation 2.2):

$$\text{true profit} = \text{accounting profit} - \text{profit grants}$$
$$TP = P - [RG + A \cdot (m - c) + DX].$$
(2.6)

All else constant, true profit is the change in retained earnings that would obtain in the absence of profit grants. Positive true profits are a social benefit because governments or donors could withdraw them from the DFI for use in other development projects. By the same logic, negative true profits (true losses) are social costs.

Although easily confused, the concept of *true profit* is distinct from the concept of *profit grants*. Profit grants are cash gifts from government or donors recorded as revenue. Profit grants inflate accounting profit. True profit is accounting profit after the removal of profit grants and discounts on expenses. True profit is what accounting profit would be in the absence of distortions due to access to public funds.

## What Is the Formula of the Subsidy Dependence Index?

Yaron (1992a) defines the SDI as subsidy *S* divided by revenue from loans $LP \cdot i$, where *LP* is the average loan portfolio and *i* is the yield on loans:

$$
\begin{aligned}
\text{SDI} &= \frac{\text{subsidy}}{\text{revenue from lending}} \\
&= \frac{S}{LP \cdot i}.
\end{aligned}
$$
(2.7)

The SDI is the percentage change in the yield on loans (or, equivalently, in revenue from loans) that, all else constant, would make subsidy zero. For example, an SDI of 1.00 means that an increase in the yield of 100 percent would wipe out subsidy and make the SDI equal zero. An SDI of zero or less means the DFI could compensate society for its opportunity cost and still show a profit. It also means that the Subsidy-Adjusted ROE would exceed the social opportunity cost.

## What Is the Denominator of the Subsidy Dependence Index?

The denominator of the SDI is revenue from loans. This is the product of the average loan portfolio outstanding *LP* and the yield on loans *i*:

revenue from loans = average loan portfolio · yield on loans
$$= LP \cdot i.$$
(2.8)

The yield $i$ is interest and fee revenue from loans, divided by the average loan portfolio:

$$i = \frac{\text{interest and fees from loans}}{\text{average loan portfolio}}.$$
(2.9)

## What Is the Numerator of the Subsidy Dependence Index?

Yaron (1992a) defines the numerator of the SDI as subsidy $S$:

$$S = m \cdot E + A \cdot (m - c) + K - P$$
(2.10)

where $S$ is subsidy, $m$ is the social opportunity cost, $E$ is average equity, $A$ is average public debt, $c$ is the rate paid for public debt, $K$ is revenue grants and discounts on expenses, and $P$ is accounting profit. Subsidy is the sum of the opportunity cost of the funds lodged in the net worth of a DFI and of the three types of profit grants, less the accounting profits the DFI could use to compensate for opportunity costs while still showing a profit. This monograph assumes that all net worth in average equity $E$ comes from public sources. $K$ is "the sum of all other annual subsidies received by the DFI (such as partial or complete coverage of the DFI's operational costs by the state) . . . [and] all other miscellaneous subsidies that a DFI might receive. These include subsidization of training costs, free use of government facilities and vehicles, free computer facilities, full or partial exemption from the deposit reserve requirement, and full or partial guarantee by the state of loan repayment by subborrowers in default" (Yaron 1992b, pp. 6, 12). In other words, $K$ is revenue grants plus discounts on expenses:

$$K = RG + DX.$$
(2.11)

Clarity about $K$ matters because if $K$ does not include revenue grants, then the SDI will depend on the arbitrary form of subsidized funds. Worse, the SDI would underestimate subsidy. Two recent attempts to adjust the SDI (chapter 5) botch $K$.

Given $K$ (equation 2.11), the level of subsidy $S$ (equation 2.10) is:

$$S = m \cdot E + A \cdot (m - c) + RG + DX - P.$$
(2.12)

Given year-end financial statements and assuming that stocks grow and flows occur at a constant pace through the year, average stocks are half the sum of the start and end stocks. The end stock of equity is the start stock plus the change in the stock:

$$E = (E_0 + E_1)/2$$
$$= (E_0 + E_0 + \Delta E)/2 \qquad (2.13)$$
$$= E_0 + (1/2) \cdot \Delta E.$$

The change in equity $\Delta E$ is the sum of flows of the six forms of subsidized funds:

$$\Delta E = equity\ grants + profit\ grants$$
$$= DG + PC + RG + A \cdot (m - c) + DX + TP. \qquad (2.14)$$

We rewrite the formula for subsidy (equation 2.10) with the formula for true profits (equation 2.6), $K$ (equation 2.11), average equity $E$ (equation 2.13), and the change in equity $\Delta E$ (equation 2.14):

$$S = m \cdot E + A \cdot (m - c) + K - P$$
$$= m \cdot [E_0 + (1/2) \cdot (DG + PC + RG + A \cdot (m - c) + DX + TP)]$$
$$+ RG + A \cdot (m - c) + DX - [TP + RG + A \cdot (m - c) + DX] \qquad (2.15)$$
$$= m \cdot E_0 + (m/2) \cdot [DG + PC + RG + A \cdot (m - c) + DX + TP] - TP.$$

This breaks the SDI into three terms. The first term, $m \cdot E_0$, is the opportunity cost of the subsidized funds that the DFI used through the whole year. The second term, $(m/2) \cdot [DG + PC + RG + A \cdot (m - c) + DX + TP]$, is the opportunity cost of the fresh subsidized funds that the DFI got in the course of the year. On average—or in the absence of knowledge of the times when flows of public funds were received—the DFI had the use of half the change in the stock of these new funds. The third term, $TP$, is the true profit that the DFI would record without subsidies, what the DFI could use to compensate society if it had no profit grants. Subsidy $S$ is then equal to the unpaid social opportunity cost less profit generated from operations.

The formula also shows that the SDI does not depend on the form of subsidized funds. Total subsidized funds from past years (in $E_0$) have a marginal and average cost of $m$. Total fresh subsidized funds have an average cost of $(m/2)$.

## Why Does the Subsidy Dependence Index Compare Subsidy to Revenue from Loans?

The key of the SDI is the measurement of subsidy. The comparison of subsidy to revenue from loans is important, but secondary. Many things affect subsidy, and subsidy could be compared with any item from the financial statements. Yaron (1994) focuses not only on revenue from loans but also on loan recuperation, deposit mobilization, and administrative costs. The choice to focus first on revenue from loans makes sense for four reasons.

First, DFIs often set interest rates by decree or have rates set for them by governments or donors. Within a range, the DFI can often change them with a stroke of a pen. In theory, interest rate hikes can dampen demand and prompt loan losses (Morduch 2000; Stiglitz and Weiss 1981). In practice, few DFIs have doused demand or spawned a rash of default with higher interest rates because demand outstrips supply (Rosenberg 1996) (box 2.2; figures 2.2, 2.3). An efficient DFI does not gouge when it charges enough to cover its costs in the long term.

Iqbal (1986) found that interest rates mattered much less to small farmers than to big farmers. According to Singh, Squire, and Strauss (1986, p. 175):

> It follows that the elimination or reduction of subsidies to programs providing agricultural credit may serve the dual purpose of increasing efficiency in the capital market and simultaneously improving equity, since the reduction in borrowing by "large" farmers will exceed that by "small" ones.

Second, if public funds will be cut in the long term, then the chances of survival increase as a DFI can cover more of the cost of private funds with revenues from loans.

Third, revenue from loans is the biggest item in the income statement and usually exceeds all other operational sources of income combined. Most DFIs cannot reduce expenses or increase nonloan income enough to compensate for subsidies, so higher prices for loans may be the best option, at least in the short term.

Fourth, the comparison of subsidy with revenue from loans places subsidy in the context of the size of the DFI. Measures of effective protection or of domestic resource cost do the same thing (Tweeten 1992; Gittinger 1982). The comparison also allows the SDI to be seen as the matching grant society provides the DFI (subsidy in the numerator of the SDI) for each dollar of revenue from interest and fees earned from loans to clients in the target group (the denominator of the SDI).

## Could Subsidy Be Compared to Anything Else?

Subsidy can be compared with anything in units of dollars per unit of time. Good candidates are average equity or average assets. Such com-

## Box 2.2.  Real Yields at Grameen and BancoSol

Along with the *unit-desa* system of Bank Rakyat Indonesia, the most famous DFIs in the world are the Grameen Bank of Bangladesh (Hashemi 1997; Khandker 1996) and BancoSol of Bolivia (Gonzalez-Vega and others 1997; Mosley 1996). The real yield on loans at Grameen and BancoSol varied widely, but the loan portfolios grew consistently and default stayed low. Thus, there may be room to increase interest rates and/or fees in the pursuit of subsidy independence.

From 1984 to 1994, Grameen earned a nominal yield that varied from 12 to 19 percent (figure 2.2). Inflation varied from 1 to 22 percent, and the real yield varied from –1 to 14 percent. More than 99 percent of taka disbursed were recovered (Schreiner 1999b), and the loan portfolio grew from $9 million to $275 million. The portfolio grew and default was low despite big changes in the real yield.

From 1987 to 1996, the nominal yield at BancoSol varied from 36 to 63 percent (figure 2.3). Inflation varied from 8 to 23 percent, and the real yield varied from 11 to 49 percent. More than 99 percent of dollars disbursed were recovered, and the loan portfolio grew from 0 to $47 million (Schreiner 1997). Again, huge swings in the real yield went side-by-side with huge portfolio growth and low default.

### Figure 2.2.  Grameen: Inflation and Nominal and Real Yields

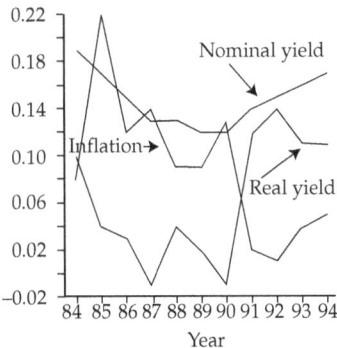

### Figure 2.3.  BancoSol: Inflation and Nominal and Real Yields

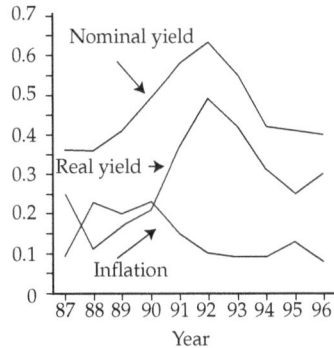

*Sources:* Schreiner (1997); Yaron, Benjamin, and Piprek (1997); Khandker, Khalily, and Khan (1995); Hashemi (1997); and IMF (various years).

parisons result in a Subsidy-Adjusted Return on Equity (SAROE) or a Subsidy-Adjusted Return on Assets (SAROA). If subsidy is less than zero, then the SAROE will exceed its hurdle rate, the social opportunity cost.

A DFI might respond to the loss of subsidy or might decrease its subsidy dependence in many ways (Yaron 1992b). For example, it could slash administrative costs, dun borrowers more, grow the loan portfolio, or boost productivity.

All these strategies require care and analysis. Also, the DFI is a price-taker in its investment portfolio, and so it cannot increase those revenues much without an increase in risk. Comparisons with the average loan portfolio *LP* require care because the DFI cannot increase *LP* with the same ease as interest rates. Rapid growth in loan volume seems more likely to provoke a rash of default than would a rapid price increase because rapid growth in the short term can only be achieved by accepting lower-quality clients.

## Does the Subsidy Dependence Index Prescribe Interest Rate Hikes?

The SDI does not prescribe interest rate hikes; rather, the SDI describes social cost and how much yields would have to increase—all else constant—to eliminate subsidy.

The SDI does not condemn subsidies nor public DFIs; after all, they may be the best way to improve social welfare. But society should pursue knowledge of the cost of DFIs to check whether they are good stewards of public funds. Governments and donors should not buy DFIs sight unseen nor measure their performance with inappropriate tools. Of course, they also need some estimate of benefits to check the social worth of DFIs.

## Numerical Examples of the Subsidy Dependence Index

The following describes the financial results of an example DFI and then walks through the calculation of the SDI. The DFI was born on January 1 of Year 01, and the averages for Year 01 use the figures (all zero) for the end of Year 00.

### Description of Financial Results for Year 01

In the balance sheet of the first year of the example DFI (table 2.2), most assets (more than two-thirds) are loans (lines Ad and Ag), and investments and fixed assets are modest. Cash is 20 percent of all assets. Half of all liabilities are public debt, and half are deposits and private debt (lines

Ah, Ai, and Aj). While governments or donors own some shares (line Al), most net worth comes from direct grants (line Am). The example DFI is highly subsidized.

The first-year income statement (table 2.3) shows that the DFI paid 25 in interest for its liabilities (line Bg), spent 600 in operating costs (line Bj), and did not provide for loan losses (line Bi). Revenues from loans and investments were 420 + 5 = 425 (lines Ba, Bb, and Bc). Operating revenue less operating costs and financial costs produced an operating margin of 425 − (25 + 600) = −200 (line Bk). This would have been even more negative in the absence of the discount on expenses of 100 (line Bn). As it was, this and a revenue grant of 400 (line Bl) let the example DFI boast an accounting profit of 200 (line Bm).

If gifts from discounts on expenses and revenue grants of 100 + 400 = 500 were called equity grants rather than profit grants, then accounting profits would be negative. Thus, measures that use accounting profit can obscure the true performance of a public DFI. The accounting treatment of a gift should not change measures of business performance.

Rates of interest are ratios of revenues and expenses from the income statement to average stocks from the balance sheet. The yield on loans $i$ for the example DFI in Year 01 is $(420)/[(0 + 2{,}100)/2] = 0.40$ (line Cv of table 2.4). This result uses the formula for the yield on loans (equation 2.9), the revenue from loans (line Ba in table 2.3), and the start and end stocks of the net loan portfolio (line Ad in table 2.2).

The interest rate on public debt is $(10)/[(0 + 400)/2] = 0.05$. This uses the formula for $c$ (equation 2.4), the interest expense on public debt (line Bf in table 2.3), and the start and end stocks of public debt (line Aj of table 2.2).

With an assumed opportunity cost to society of public debt $m$ of 10 percent per year in real terms (line Ck of table 2.4), the DFI would pay $(0.10) \cdot [(0 + 400)/2] = 20$ for equivalent private debt. The discount on public debt is the social opportunity cost less what was actually paid, $20 - 10 = 10$ (line Cl).

The example DFI paid an interest rate on deposits of $(5)/[(0 + 200)/2] = 0.05$ (line He of table A.1). The interest rate paid on private debt was $(10)/[(0 + 200)/2] = 0.10$. The DFI also earned a yield on investments $j$ of $(5)/[(0 + 200)/2] = 0.05$.

## What Is the Subsidy Dependence Index of the Example Development Finance Institution for Year 01?

The SDI of the example DFI for Year 01 was 100 percent (line Cx of table 2.4). Table 2.4 uses the received formula for subsidy (equation 2.10), but the alternative formula (equation 2.15) gives the same result (line Dq of table 2.5). An SDI of 100 percent means that, all else constant, an

**Table 2.2. Balance Sheet**

| Line | | | 12/31/01 | 12/31/02 | 12/31/03 |
|---|---|---|---|---|---|
| | **Assets** | | | | |
| Aa | Cash | Data | 600 | 700 | 800 |
| Ab | Loan portfolio (gross) | Data | 2,100 | 3,300 | 5,200 |
| Ac | Reserve for loan losses | Data | 0 | 0 | 0 |
| Ad | Loan portfolio (net), $LP$ | Ab + Ac | 2,100 | 3,300 | 5,200 |
| Ae | Investments, $I$ | Data | 200 | 400 | 600 |
| Af | Fixed assets (net) | Data | 100 | 200 | 200 |
| Ag | Total assets | Aa + Ad + Ae + Af | 3,000 | 4,600 | 6,800 |
| | **Liabilities** | | | | |
| Ah | Deposit liabilities | Data | 200 | 400 | 600 |
| Ai | Private debt | Data | 200 | 300 | 400 |
| Aj | Public debt, $A$ | Data | 400 | 800 | 1,200 |
| Ak | Total liabilities | Ah + Ai + Aj | 800 | 1,500 | 2,200 |
| | **Equity** | | | | |
| Al | Paid-in capital, $PC$ | Data | 300 | 645 | 910 |
| Am | Direct grants, $DG$ | Data | 1,700 | 2,000 | 2,300 |
| An | Retained earnings | $An_{t-1}$ + Bm | 200 | 455 | 1,390 |
| Ao | Total equity | Al + Am + An | 2,200 | 3,100 | 4,600 |
| Ap | Total equity and liabilities | Ak + Ao | 3,000 | 4,600 | 6,800 |

*Note:* Monetary figures in constant units.
*Source:* Example of authors.

34

**Table 2.3. Income Statement**

| Line | | | 12/31/01 | 12/31/02 | 12/31/03 |
|------|------|------|----------|----------|----------|
| Ba | Revenue from loans, $LP \cdot i$ | Data | 420 | 1,080 | 1,700 |
| Bb | Revenue from investments, $I \cdot j$ | Data | 5 | 15 | 25 |
| Bc | Total revenue operations | Ba + Bb | 425 | 1,095 | 1,725 |
| Bd | Exp. int. deposit liabilities | Data | 5 | 15 | 25 |
| Be | Exp. int. private debt | Data | 10 | 25 | 35 |
| Bf | Interest expense on public debt, $A \cdot c$ | Data | 10 | 30 | 50 |
| Bg | Total int. exp. | Bd + Be + Bf | 25 | 70 | 110 |
| Bh | Financial margin | Bc – Bg | 400 | 1,025 | 1,615 |
| Bi | Exp. prov. reserve for loan losses | Data | 0 | 0 | 0 |
| Bj | Exp. admin. | Data | 600 | 1,170 | 1,080 |
| Bk | Operating margin | Bh – (Bi + Bj) | (200) | (145) | 535 |
| Bl | Rev. grants, $RG$ | Data | 400 | 400 | 400 |
| Bm | Accounting profit, $P$ | Bk + Bl | 200 | 255 | 935 |
| | **Memo item:** | | | | |
| Bn | Discounts on expenses, $DX$ | Data | 100 | 100 | 100 |

*Note:* Monetary figures in constant units.
*Source:* Example of authors.

**Table 2.4. Calculation of the Subsidy Dependence Index**

| Line | | | 12/31/01 | 12/31/02 | 12/31/03 |
|---|---|---|---|---|---|
| Ca | Start equity | $Al_{t-1} + Am_{t-1} + An$ | 0 | 2,200 | 3,100 |
| Cb | End equity | $Al + Am + An$ | 2,200 | 3,100 | 4,600 |
| Cc | Average equity, $E$ | $(Ca + Cb)/2$ | 1,100 | 2,650 | 3,850 |
| Cd | Opportunity cost of society, $m$ | Data | 0.10 | 0.10 | 0.10 |
| Ce | Subsidy on equity, $E \cdot m$ | $Cc \cdot Cd$ | 110 | 265 | 385 |
| Cf | Start public debt | $Aj_{t-1}$ | 0 | 400 | 800 |
| Cg | End public debt | $Aj$ | 400 | 800 | 1,200 |
| Ch | Average public debt, $A$ | $(Cf + Cg)/2$ | 200 | 600 | 1,000 |
| Ci | Exp. int. public debt, $A \cdot c$ | Bf | 10 | 30 | 50 |
| Cj | Rate paid for public debt, $c$ | Ci/Ch | 0.05 | 0.05 | 0.05 |
| Ck | Opportunity cost public debt, $m$ | Data | 0.10 | 0.10 | 0.10 |
| Cl | Discount on public debt, $A \cdot (m - c)$ | $Ch \cdot (Ck - Cj)$ | 10 | 30 | 50 |
| Cm | Revenue grants, $RG$ | Bl | 400 | 400 | 400 |
| Cn | Discounts on expenses, $DX$ | Bn | 100 | 100 | 100 |
| Co | Revenue grants and discounts on expenses, $K$ | $Cm + Cn$ | 500 | 500 | 500 |

| | | | | | |
|---|---|---|---|---|---|
| Cp | Accounting profit, $P$ | Bm | 200 | 255 | 935 |
| Cq | Subsidy, $S$ | Ce + Cl + Co − Cp | 420 | 540 | 0 |
| Cr | Start loan portfolio (net) | $Ad_{t-1}$ | 0 | 2,100 | 3,300 |
| Cs | End loan portfolio (net) | Ad | 2,100 | 3,300 | 5,200 |
| Ct | Average loan portfolio (net), $LP$ | (Cr + Cs)/2 | 1,050 | 2,700 | 4,250 |
| Cu | Revenue from loans, $LP \cdot i$ | Ba | 420 | 1,080 | 1,700 |
| Cv | Yield on lending, $i$ | Cu/Ct | 0.40 | 0.40 | 0.40 |
| Cw | Revenue from lending, $LP \cdot i$ | Ct · Cv | 420 | 1,080 | 1,700 |
| Cx | Subsidy Dependence Index, $S/(LP \cdot i)$ | Cq/Cw | 1.00 | 0.50 | 0.00 |
| Cy | Yield on lending, $i$ | Cv | 0.40 | 0.40 | 0.40 |
| Cz | Change in yield | Cy · Cx | 0.40 | 0.20 | 0.00 |
| Caa | Subsidy-free yield | Cy + Cz | 0.80 | 0.60 | 0.40 |

Note: Monetary figures in constant units. Average equity includes profit.
Source: Example of authors.

**Table 2.5. Alternative Calculation of the Subsidy Dependence Index**

| Line | | | 12/31/01 | 12/31/02 | 12/31/03 |
|------|---|---|---------|---------|---------|
| Da | Opportunity cost of society, $m$ | Cd | 0.10 | 0.10 | 0.10 |
| Db | Start equity, $E_0$ | Ca | 0 | 2,200 | 3,100 |
| Dc | $E_0 \cdot m$ | Da · Db | 0 | 220 | 310 |
| Dd | End direct grants | Am | 1,700 | 2,000 | 2,300 |
| De | Start direct grants | $Am_{t-1}$ | 0 | 1,700 | 2,000 |
| Df | Change direct grants, $DG$ | Dd – De | 1,700 | 300 | 300 |
| Dg | End paid-in capital | Al | 300 | 645 | 910 |
| Dh | Start paid-in capital | $Al_{t-1}$ | 0 | 300 | 645 |
| Di | Change paid-in capital, $PC$ | Dg – Dh | 300 | 345 | 265 |
| Dj | Discount public debt, $A \cdot (m - c)$ | Cl | 10 | 30 | 50 |
| Dk | Rev. grants, $RG$ | Bl | 400 | 400 | 400 |
| Dl | Discounts on expenses, $DX$ | Bn | 100 | 100 | 100 |
| Dm | Accounting profit, $P$ | Bm | 200 | 255 | 935 |
| Dn | True profit, $TP$ | Dm – (Dj + Dk + Dl) | (310) | (275) | 385 |
| Do | Subsidy, $S$ | Dc + (Da/2) · (Df + Di + Dj + Dk – Dl + Dn) – Dn | 420 | 540 | 0 |
| Dp | Rev. from loans, $LP \cdot i$ | Ba | 420 | 1,080 | 1,700 |
| Dq | Subsidy Dependence Index, $S/(LP \cdot i)$ | Do/Dp | 1.00 | 0.50 | 0.00 |

*Note:* Monetary figures in constant units. Average equity includes profit.
*Source:* Example of authors.

increase of 100 percent in the yield on loans would allow the DFI to show a profit and still compensate for the social opportunity cost of its funds.

The subsidy on equity is $1,100 \cdot 0.10 = 110$ (line Ce of table 2.4). This is the product of an average equity $E$ of $[(0 + 0 + 0) + (300 + 1,700 + 200)]/2 = 1,100$ (line Cc) and of a social opportunity cost of equity $m$ of 10 percent (line Cd).

The discount on public debt (line Cl) is $[(0 + 400)/2] \cdot (0.10 - 0.05) = 10$. This is the product of average public debt $A$ (line Ch) and of the opportunity cost to society of public debt $m$ (line Ck) less the rate paid $c$ (line Cj).

The amount $K$ (equation 2.11) is $400 + 100 = 500$ (line Co). This is the sum of revenue grants $RG$ (line Cm) and discounts on expenses $DX$ (line Cn). Accounting profit $P$ is 200 (line Cp). Finally, revenue from loans $LP \cdot i$ is $[(0 + 2,100)/2] \cdot 0.40 = 420$ (line Cw). This is the product of the average loan portfolio $LP$ (line Ct) and the yield on loans $i$ (line Cv). Thus, the SDI for Year 01 is (equation 2.7):

$$
\begin{aligned}
\text{SDI}_{01} &= \frac{S}{LP \cdot i} \\
&= \frac{m \cdot E + A \cdot (m - c) + K - P}{LP \cdot i} \\
&= \frac{0.10 \cdot 1,100 + 200 \cdot (0.10 - 0.05) + 500 - 200}{1,050 \cdot 0.40} \qquad (2.16) \\
&= (110 + 10 + 500 - 200)/420 \\
&= 420/420 = 1.00.
\end{aligned}
$$

## What Does the Subsidy Dependence Index for Year 01 Mean?

All else constant, the SDI for Year 01 of 100 percent means the DFI could compensate for the social opportunity cost of its funds and still show a profit if revenue from loans increased by 100 percent. If the size of the loan portfolio does not change, then this would mean doubling the yield. In general,

$$
\begin{aligned}
\text{Subsidy-free yield} &= \text{actual yield} \cdot (1 + \text{SDI}) \\
&= \text{actual yield} + \text{implied change in yield.}
\end{aligned} \qquad (2.17)
$$

The SDI is a relative measure; it measures the implied change in the yield that would compensate for subsidies, relative to the actual yield. The actual yield varies from year to year and from DFI to DFI. Also, the nominal yield varies with inflation even if the real yield does not. Thus, good analysis will consider, in both real and nominal terms, the absolute level of subsidy $S$ (a dollar amount), the ratio of subsidy to revenue from loans (the SDI, a percentage), the actual yield $i$ (a percentage), the implied change in the yield (a percentage), and the subsidy-free yield (a percentage). In this example, the actual yield is 40 percent (line Cy in table 2.4). The subsidy-free yield is $0.40 + 0.40 \cdot 1.00 = 0.80$ (line Caa). The implied change is $0.80 - 0.40 = 0.40$ (line Cz). Because inflation is assumed to be zero, the real yield equals the nominal yield.

## Does the Subsidy Dependence Index Depend on How Average Equity Is Defined?

Like ROE, the SDI depends on how average equity is defined. Accountants do not agree on the best way to define average equity. All agree that average equity should include start equity $E_0$ and fresh injections to equity such as equity grants and paid-in capital in the year, weighted for the time of injection. Average equity should also include revenue grants $RG$, the discount on public debt $A \cdot (m - c)$, and the discount on expenses $DX$ because these profit grants are equity grants in disguise. Opinion differs, however, whether average equity should also include true profit in the current year. When average equity excludes true profit in the current year, then the measure of subsidy in the SDI more closely resembles a present-value measure. For this reason, it is preferable to exclude true profit in the current year from measures of average equity.

As in Yaron (1992a, 1992b), the formulae in this monograph include true profit $TP$ in average equity (e.g., equation 2.15). This recognizes that owners could, in principle, withdraw true profit as it accrues. If they choose not to, then it is as if they withdrew true profit but injected it back as paid-in capital. If average equity includes true profit, then the measure does not depend on this arbitrary choice made by owners. Also, the use of average equity can be seen as a practical solution to imperfect data without knowledge of the timing of injections to equity, accrual of profit, and dividend pay-outs. The use of start equity would be more consistent with economic paradigms based on net present cost, but this approach would require more accurate data than are normally available to external analysts. The use of average equity rather than start equity is a compromise necessitated by the available data.

Unfortunately, this definition of average equity is inconsistent with the way some other rates are measured. For example, suppose that a DFI has a constant balance through a year of 100 of debt and 100 of paid-in capital. Suppose that in a year the DFI pays 10 in interest for the debt and that it accrues a true profit of 10. The common way to measure the rate of interest on the debt is as $10/[(100 + 100)/2] = 0.10$. At the same time, the rate of Return on Equity with true profit included in average equity is $10/[(100 + 100 + 10)/2] = 0.095$. These two measures are inconsistent.

This can be reconciled in two ways. The first recognizes that the interest on the debt was paid throughout the year and not just at the end, so the DFI had to finance the interest with 10 of debt. Then the measure of the interest rate on debt is $10/[(100 + 100 + 10)/2] = 0.095$, the same as the common way to measure rates of Return on Equity.

The second way to reconcile the measures is to assume that owners measure their returns not on average funds used but rather on start funds invested. This is similar to the practice of measuring the effective annual interest rate on a loan as if its balance did not change in the course of a year. In this case, the measure of the rate of Return on Equity is $10/[(100 + 100)/2] = 0.10$, the same as the common way to measure rates of interest on debt.

The method used to measure average equity affects the SDI (Schreiner 1997; Yaron 1992b). The choice of method matters more as the absolute value of true profit grows relative to start equity (box 2.3). For the example DFI in Year 01, suppose that average equity does not include true profit. Thus, average equity does not change when the yield on loans doubles and when true profit increases by 420. The new SDI is:

$$
\begin{aligned}
\text{SDI}'_{01} &= \frac{0.10 \cdot 1{,}100 + 200 \cdot (0.10 - 0.05) + 500 - (200 + 420)}{1{,}050 \cdot [0.40 \cdot (1 + 1.00)]} \\
&= \frac{110 + 10 + 500 - 620}{840} \\
&= 0/840 = 0.
\end{aligned}
\tag{2.18}
$$

If the change in true profit does affect average equity, then the new SDI is:

$$
\begin{aligned}
\text{SDI}''_{01} &= \frac{0.10 \cdot (1{,}100 + 200) + 200 \cdot (0.10 - 0.05) + 500 - (200 + 420)}{1{,}050 \cdot [0.40 \cdot (1 + 1.00)]} \\
&= \frac{130 + 10 + 500 - 620}{840} \\
&= 20/840 \doteq 0.02.
\end{aligned}
\tag{2.19}
$$

### What Are the Subsidy Dependence Indexes for Year 02 and Year 03?

The example DFI cut its SDI in Years 02 and 03. It did not increase its yield on loans in Year 02; rather, it increased the average loan portfolio by 157 percent (line Ct of table 2.4) while administrative costs increased only 95 percent (line Bj of table 2.3). In short, the DFI got more efficient. Perhaps costs were high in the first year because the DFI was born with all it would ever need. It bought office space, hired a full complement of administrators, set up a computer system, and hired

## Box 2.3.  The Subsidy Dependence Index and Average Equity at Bank Rakyat Indonesia

The case of the *unit-desa* system of Bank Rakyat Indonesia illustrates the sensitivity of the SDI and ROE to the inclusion of current-year profit in the measure of average equity $E$ (Charitonenko, Patten, and Yaron 1998).

The stock of equity in the *unit-desa* system at the start of 1995 $E_0$ was about 72 billion rupiah ($1 was worth about 2,200 rupiah). Accounting profits $P$ in 1995 were about 393 billion rupiah. Thus, ROE computed in terms of start equity $E_0$ was $393/72 \doteq 5.45$, or about 545 percent. With profits in the year included in the measure of average equity, ROE was $393/[(72 + 393)/2] \doteq 1.69$, or about 169 percent. Thus, the inclusion of current-year profits in equity had a large effect on the estimate of ROE.

To compute the SDI, note that the value of $K$—including discounts due to exemption from reserve requirements—was –43 billion. The *unit-desa* system used no subsidized debt, so the discount on public debt $A \cdot (m - c)$ was zero. The social opportunity cost $m$ used in Charitonenko, Patten, and Yaron (1998) was 17.9 percent, and revenue from loans $LP \cdot i$ was 861 billion rupiah.

With the inclusion of current-year profits in average equity $L$, the SDI was:

$$\{[(E_0 + E_1)/2] \cdot m + A \cdot (m - c) + K - P\}/LP \cdot i$$
$$= \{[(72+72+393)/2] \cdot 0.179 + 0 + (-43)-393]/861$$
$$\doteq -388/861$$
$$\doteq -0.45.$$

That is, the *unit-desa* system could have reduced the yield on loans by 45 percent (from about 32 percent to about 17 percent), compensated for the social opportunity cost of its public funds, and still shown a profit. This extremely high level of subsidy independence is one reason why Charitonenko, Patten, and Yaron (1997, p. 5) conclude that "no other successful, sustainable micro or rural finance institution shows the extent of outreach or the degree of financial self-sustainability that the BRI *Unit Desa* system has achieved."

What if the measurement of average equity $E$ excludes current profits? The SDI is then:

$$\{[(72 + 72)/2] \cdot 0.179 + 0 + (-43) - 393]/861 \doteq -423/861$$
$$\doteq -0.49.$$

Subsidy independence increases, although the change is only about four percentage points. Given the extremely high leverage of the *unit-desa* system (equity in 1995 was only 1.4 percent of assets) and its extremely high profitability (ROA in 1995 was 6.1 percent), the SDI does not seem very sensitive to the inclusion or exclusion of current-year profits in the measurement of average equity.

several loan officers. It took time for the loan officers to get up to speed with a full portfolio. In the meantime, costs per unit of output were high because the costs of the infrastructure were spread over a small portfolio.

Discounts on expenses $DX$ did not change (line Bn of table 2.3), and discounts on public debt tripled (line Cl of table 2.4). Average equity increased by 140 percent (line Cc of table 2.4). The SDI was cut in half:

$$
\begin{aligned}
\text{SDI}_{02} &= \frac{m \cdot E + A \cdot (m - c) + K - P}{LP \cdot i} \\
&= \frac{0.10 \cdot 2{,}650 + 600 \cdot (0.10 - 0.05) + 500 - 255}{2{,}700 \cdot 0.40} \\
&= (265 + 30 + 500 - 255)/1{,}080 \\
&= 540/1{,}080 = 0.50.
\end{aligned}
\tag{2.20}
$$

Subsidy $S$ rose from 420 to 540, but the SDI fell (lines Cq and Cx of table 2.4). The subsidy-free yield was $0.40 \cdot (1 + 0.50) = 0.60$ (line Caa), and the implied change was 0.20 (line Cz).

In the third year, the average portfolio grew by more than 50 percent (line Ct of table 2.4). Administrative expenses fell by about 8 percent (line Bj of table 2.3). Discounts on expenses $DX$ did not change. Discounts on public debt grew by 20 (line Cl of table 2.4). The example DFI still got fresh flows of all six forms of subsidized funds, but increased profits drove the SDI to zero:

$$
\begin{aligned}
\text{SDI}_{03} &= \frac{m \cdot E + A \cdot (m - c) + K - P}{LP \cdot i} \\
&= \frac{0.10 \cdot 3{,}850 + 1{,}000 \cdot (0.10 - 0.05) + 500 - 935}{4{,}250 \cdot 0.40} \\
&= (385 + 50 + 500 - 935)/1{,}700 \\
&= 0/1{,}700 = 0.00.
\end{aligned}
\tag{2.21}
$$

Of course, similar examples could be presented in which the measure of equity $E$ does not include profit in the current period.

## Is Subsidy in the Subsidy Dependence Index Related to a Subsidy-Adjusted Return on Equity?

The measure of subsidy in the SDI is closely related to a Subsidy-Adjusted ROE. This is useful because ROE is the most common measure of the financial performance of a private firm. Most users of financial information know and understand ROE. ROE compares accounting profit (after tax) with average equity:

$$\text{ROE} = \frac{\text{accounting profit (after tax)}}{\text{average equity}}. \qquad (2.22)$$

ROA resembles ROE except it compares accounting profit with average assets:

$$\text{ROA} = \frac{\text{accounting profit (after tax)}}{\text{average assets}}. \qquad (2.23)$$

ROA is a useful tool for comparisons between peers in the same macroeconomic environments because it removes the effects of financial leverage. Barltrop and McNaughton (1992) and Mould (1987) explain the use of ROE, ROA, and other common financial ratios in the analysis of DFIs.

ROE and ROA use accounting profits, and accounting profits depend on whether a gift is called an equity grant or a profit grant. A Subsidy-Adjusted ROE (SAROE) (or a Subsidy-Adjusted ROA [SAROA]) would replace accounting profit with true profit. An SAROE compares true profits with average equity:

$$\text{SAROE} = \frac{\text{true profit}}{\text{average equity}}. \qquad (2.24)$$

Likewise, an SAROA compares true profit with average assets. The SAROE and the SAROA are useful to compare public DFIs with peers (Christen 1997). Peer comparisons are the standard way to benchmark the performance of banks (Barltrop and McNaughton 1992; Koch 1992).

The SDI and the SAROE are closely related. Yaron (1992b, p. 5) hints at this when he says that subsidy is less than zero when "the Return on Equity, net of any subsidy received, equals or exceeds the opportunity cost of funds." The SDI is negative if and only if the SAROE exceeds the social opportunity cost.

The proof that a negative SDI implies an SAROE higher than the hurdle rate—that is, the opportunity cost of funds—uses the alternative formula for subsidy (equation 2.15), the formula for the change in equity (equation 2.14), and the formula for average equity (equation 2.13):

$$
\begin{aligned}
S &= m \cdot E_0 + (m/2) \cdot [DG + PC + RG + A \cdot (m - c) + DX + TP] - TP \\
&= m \cdot E_0 + m \cdot (1/2) \cdot \Delta E - TP \\
&= m \cdot [E_0 + (1/2) \cdot \Delta E] - TP \\
&= m \cdot E - TP.
\end{aligned}
\qquad (2.25)
$$

This simple formula shows that subsidy $S$ is the opportunity cost of the equity used in a year less what the DFI could have paid for that equity and still shown a true profit. A negative SDI implies an SAROE above the social hurdle rate:

$$S \leq 0$$
$$m \cdot E - TP \leq 0$$
$$m \cdot E \leq TP \tag{2.26}$$
$$m \leq TP/E$$

opportunity cost of capital $\leq$ Subsidy-Adjusted ROE.

A strength of the SDI is that it answers the same question as an SAROE. Figure 2.4 compares ROE and SAROE for the example DFI (table 2.6). In the three years, ROE goes from 0.18 to 0.10 to 0.24. ROE seems to show that performance improved in the second year and worsened in the third. In contrast, SAROE goes from –0.28 to –0.10 to 0.10, showing that improvement was constant. This shows that ROE is not a good measure of the financial performance of subsidized DFIs. By the third year (when the SDI was zero), the DFI could have compensated society for its opportunity cost and still have shown a profit. ROA and SAROA follow the same pattern as ROE and SAROE (figure 2.5).

If the measure of subsidy in the SDI and the SAROE gives the same answer for one question, then why use the SDI? After all, the process of adjusting the financial statements as required to compute the SAROE helps to ensure that all standard, widely understood financial ratios are meaningful. The SDI, however, is more than just the measure of subsidy in its numerator, and thus the SDI has at least three features that the SAROE does not. First, subsidy independence is zero with the SDI but $m$ with the SAROE. Given human psychology, naïve users may celebrate a positive SAROE even if it is still less than $m$. The chances that the SAROE is positive and yet less than $m$ increase in low-income countries where inflation may be high and where real interest rates tend to be high due to the underdevelopment of the financial sector. Second, the SDI is a measure of the matching grant provided by society (the numerator) for each dollar of interest paid by the clients of a DFI (the denominator). For example, if the SDI of a DFI is 1.00, then the SDI contrasts the dollar provided by society with the dollar provided by the client in a way that the SAROE does not. Thus, the SDI allows analysts to compare the matching grant provided to the target group through a DFI with matching grants (potential or actual) provided through other channels. Third, the SDI worsens if a DFI abandons its mission and puts resources in investments other than loans to the target group, all else constant, because revenue from loans $LP \cdot i$ in the denominator decreases. The SAROE, however,

**Figure 2.4. ROE versus SAROE for the Example DFI**

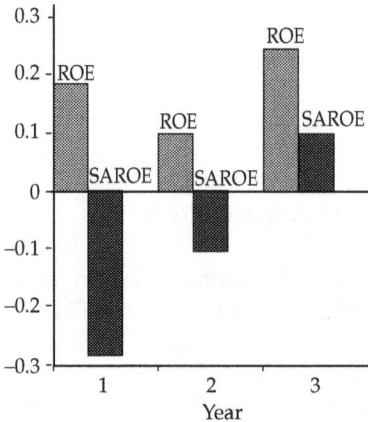

**Figure 2.5. ROA versus SAROA for the Example DFI**

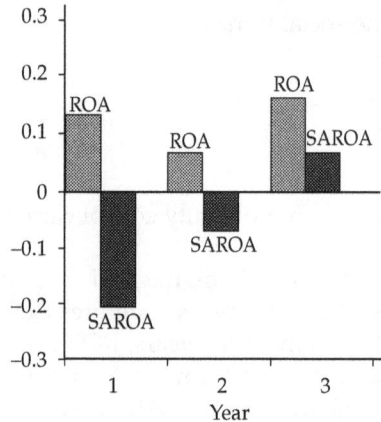

stays the same, and may even improve, if the other investments are more profitable than loans to the target group (box 2.4).

## How Does the Subsidy Dependence Index Change as Its Parts Change?

The SDI has many parts, among them the yield on loans $i$. Knowledge of how changes in these parts drive changes in the SDI may help to map concrete plans to reduce subsidy dependence.

Of course, increased subsidy independence may not always be possible or even preferred. For example, the DFI controls some parts of the SDI but not all. Still, knowledge of how social cost might be reduced is always useful to society.

The figures that follow show how the SDI for Year 01 of the example DFI changes as one of its parts changes, all else constant. The figures show the direction of change better than the level of change. The level depends on the units and on the levels of the part being changed as well as the units and levels of all other parts of the SDI.

### How Does the Subsidy Dependence Index Change as the Yield on Loans Changes?

As the yield on loans $i$ increases, the SDI decreases at a decreasing rate (figure 2.6). All else constant, an increase in $i$ increases the denominator of the SDI because it increases revenue from loans. This decreases the

**Table 2.6. ROE, SAROE, ROA, and SAROA**

| Line | | | 12/31/01 | 12/31/02 | 12/31/03 |
|------|---|---|----------|----------|----------|
| Ea | Accounting profit, $P$ | Bm | 200 | 255 | 935 |
| Eb | Revenue grants, $RG$ | Bl | 400 | 400 | 400 |
| Ec | Discount on public debt, $A \cdot (m-c)$ | Cl | 10 | 30 | 50 |
| Ed | Discounts on expenses, $DX$ | Bn | 100 | 100 | 100 |
| Ee | True profit, $TP$ | Ea − (Eb + Ec + Ed) | (310) | (275) | 385 |
| Ef | Start equity | $Ao_{t-1}$ | 0 | 2,200 | 3,100 |
| Eg | End equity | Ao | 2,200 | 3,100 | 4,600 |
| Eh | Average equity, $E$ | (Ef + Eg)/2 | 1,100 | 2,650 | 3,850 |
| Ei | Start assets | $Ag_{t-1}$ | 0 | 3,000 | 4,600 |
| Ej | End assets | Ag | 3,000 | 4,600 | 6,800 |
| Ek | Average assets | (Ei + Ej)/2 | 1,500 | 3,800 | 5,700 |
| El | ROA | Ea/Ek | 0.13 | 0.07 | 0.16 |
| Em | Subsidy-Adjusted ROA | Ee/Ek | (0.21) | (0.07) | 0.07 |
| En | ROE | Ea/Eh | 0.18 | 0.10 | 0.24 |
| Eo | Subsidy-Adjusted ROE | Ee/Eh | (0.28) | (0.10) | 0.10 |

*Note:* Monetary figures in constant units. Average equity includes profit.
*Source:* Example of authors.

---

## Box 2.4. The Subsidy Dependence Index and Subsidy-Adjusted Return on Equity for an African DFI

A large African DFI illustrates how the SDI improves when funds shift away from other investments to loans to the target group, all else constant, even though the SAROE stays unchanged.

In 1998, the DFI had an average public debt $A$ of 9.91, an opportunity cost $m$ of 15.5 percent, and an actual rate paid $c$ of 3.9 percent. Average equity $E$ was 1.5, and $K$ was zero. Of the $9.91 + 1.5 = 11.41$ resources in use at the DFI, 2.47 were in the average loan portfolio $LP$, and 8.94 were invested in treasury bills. The yield on loans $i$ was 23 percent, so $LP \cdot i$ was 0.57. Finally, accounting profit $P$ was –1.42.

Thus, the SDI was $[1.5 \cdot 0.155 + 9.91 \cdot (0.155 - 0.039) + 0 - (-1.42)]/0.57 \doteq 2.8/0.57 = 492$ percent. The SAROE was $-2.8/1.5 \doteq -187$ percent, far from the hurdle rate.

With profit held constant, a shift of 1 unit from treasury bills to the loan portfolio would not affect the SAROE. The SDI, however, would improve from 492 percent to $2.8/(3.47 \cdot 0.23) \doteq 350$ percent. The SDI is more sensitive than the SAROE to the allocation of funds between loans to the target group and other investments.

*Source*: Authors.

---

SDI. The increase in $i$ also increases true profit and so decreases subsidy in the numerator (as long as $m < 200$ percent). Thus, the effects of an increase in $i$ in both the numerator and the denominator serve to decrease the SDI.

## *How Does the Subsidy Dependence Index Change as the Rate Paid on Public Debt Changes?*

If the measure of equity $E$ in the SDI includes profits in the current period, then an increase in the rate paid on public debt $c$ decreases the SDI (figure 2.7; equation 2.15). This happens because a higher rate paid for debt decreases the equity injected by the discount on public debt $A \cdot (m - c)$. In turn, this decreases the social cost of the public funds in the net worth of the DFI and so decreases the SDI. If the measure of equity $E$ does not include profit in the current period, then a change in $c$ does not affect the SDI, because the decrease in the discount on public debt $A \cdot (m - c)$ is exactly balanced by an increase in accounting profit $P$.

**Figure 2.6. The SDI and the Yield on Loans, *i***

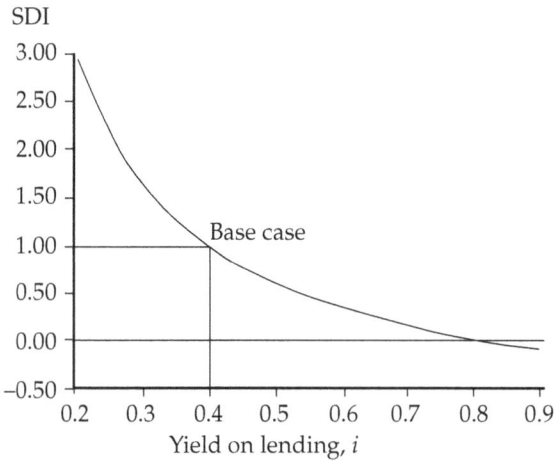

**Figure 2.7. The SDI and the Rate Paid for Public Debt, *c***

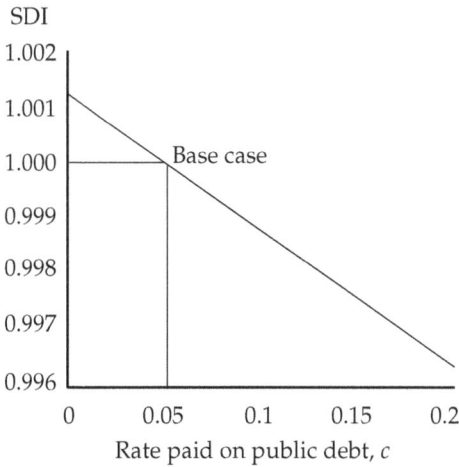

*How Does the Subsidy Dependence Index Change*
*as the Social Opportunity Cost Changes?*

The SDI increases as the social opportunity cost $m$ increases (figure 2.8). This happens in two ways. First, the increase in $m$ increases social cost through the discount on public debt $A \cdot (m - c)$ (because the spread between $m$ and $c$ widens) and decreases the ability to compensate for social cost through true profit (due to the increase in $A \cdot m$). Second, the increase in $m$ increases the social cost of the public funds in the net worth of the DFI. This is often the bulk of the social cost of a DFI.

Small changes in $m$ can lead to big changes in the SDI (figure 2.8). This is one reason why the choice of $m$ matters so much. At the same time, the fact that the SDI depends on $m$ has no policy implication for a DFI. The opportunity cost of the public funds in the DFI depends on the performance not of the DFI but of the marginal public project. (Subsidy—and the SDI—can be positive even if $m$ is zero because subsidy is the social opportunity cost of public funds used, less the ability to compensate for that cost out of true profits. If true profits are negative, then subsidy is positive even if the use of public funds has no opportunity cost.)

### How Does the Subsidy Dependence Index Change as Administrative Expenses Change?

Increases in administrative expenses decrease true profit and so increase the SDI (figure 2.9). In the first year of the example DFI, decreases in administrative expenses could make the subsidy zero. This is not always the case—social cost could be positive even if administrative costs are zero, for example, if social cost exceeds the level of administrative costs.

**Figure 2.8. The SDI and the Social Opportunity Cost, $m$**

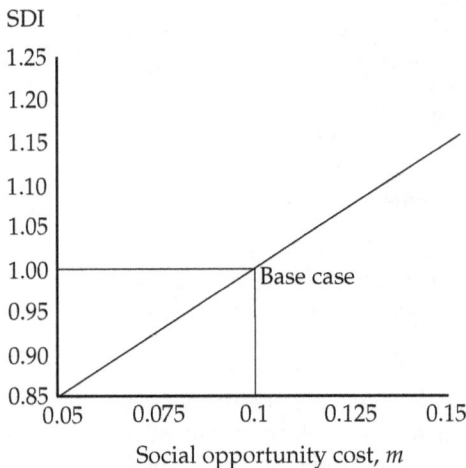

**Figure 2.9. The SDI and Administrative Expenses**

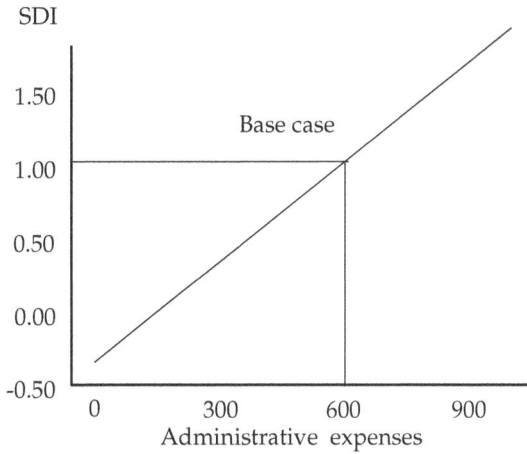

All else constant, the slope of the graph of figure 2.9 does not depend on the type of expense that changes. For example, the effect on the SDI of a $1 change in provision for loan losses is the same as the effect of a $1 change in administrative expenses. Provision for loan losses is discussed in chapter 4.

*How Does the Subsidy Dependence Index Change as Liabilities Shift from Public Debt to Deposits?*

The SDI decreases as deposits replace public debt (figure 2.10). If $d$ is the cost (both financial and administrative) of deposits, then a shift of one dollar from public debt to deposits affects subsidy $S$ in three ways. First, the shift changes the discount on public debt injected in equity by $-(m/2) \cdot (m - c)$. Because $m \geq c$, the discount is negative and so decreases subsidy. Second, the shift changes the true profit injected in equity by $(m/2) \cdot (m - d)$. True profit increases by $m$ because that is the opportunity cost of a unit of public debt, but it decreases by $d$ because that is the unit expense on deposits. Third, the switch changes the true profit available to compensate for subsidies by $(m - d)$. Because $m \geq d$, the change in true profit is positive. Because in most cases $(m/2)$ ″ 1, the net effect of the increase in true profit on subsidy is negative. Because the effect on subsidy of the decrease in the discount on public debt is also negative, a shift of one dollar from public debt to deposits decreases subsidy and thus the SDI.

**Figure 2.10.  The SDI and the Ratio of Deposits to Public Debt**

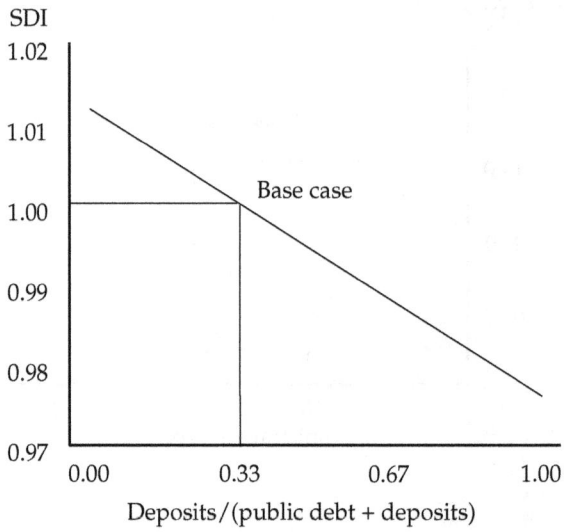

SDI

Deposits/(public debt + deposits)

# 3
# What Is a Measure of the Social Cost of a Public Development Finance Institution in the Long Term?

The $NPC_S$ is a measure of the social cost of flows of resources between society and a public DFI in any time frame. Because the SDI does not discount, it does not properly measure social cost in long time frames. Just like private investors, society should look at the present value of projects in the long term. Even if society plans to own equity for only a short time, the present value of the equity at the end of the time frame depends on expected performance after that point.

The $NPC_S$ complements short-term measures of social cost. Just like dams, DFIs should not be judged only by output in their tenth year but rather by discounted costs and benefits in their whole lifetimes.

## How Does the Net Present Cost to Society Discount Flows?

### What Is the Discount Rate?

The $NPC_S$ discounts flows by when they take place in time. The discount rate is the price of gains and costs in the present in terms of gains and costs in the future. The social discount rate $\delta_1$ for a flow one year past the start of the time frame is one divided by one plus the social opportunity cost in the first year, $m_1$ (Gittinger 1982).

This assumes that all flows take place at the end of the year. Often the analyst has year-end financial statements and assumes that flows and changes in stocks take place at a constant pace in the course of the year. In this case, flows are discounted as if they took place halfway through the year. For year $t$ in time frames that last more than one year, the discount rate for a flow or a change in a stock would be:

$$\delta_t^{t-0.5} = \left(\frac{1}{1+m_t}\right)^{1-0.5} \cdot \prod_{j=1}^{t-1}\left(\frac{1}{1+m_j}\right). \qquad (3.1)$$

The subscript $t$ is a time index. Likewise, the superscript $t - 0.5$ is not an exponent but a label. The opportunity cost $m$ may change through time.

## What Is the Formula of the Net Present Cost to Society?

Outflows from society to a DFI are social costs, and inflows back to society from a DFI are social gains. As a cost measure, the $NPC_S$ adds discounted outflows and subtracts discounted inflows. Like all discounted measures, the $NPC_S$ ignores flows sunk before the start of the time frame. As presented here, the $NPC_S$ assumes all equity injections come from society, but this assumption can be relaxed (Schreiner 1997).

The stock of equity at the start of the time frame $E_0$ is not a sunk flow. At time 0, society chooses to keep this net worth in a DFI rather than withdraw it for use elsewhere. Thus, society counts $E_0$ as an outflow:

$$NPC_S \text{ start net worth} = \delta_0^0 \cdot E_0 = E_0. \qquad (3.2)$$

After the start of the time frame, the DFI builds net worth from fresh flows of funds $FF_t$ from grants, paid-in capital, and discounts. The discounted cost of these outflows from society to the DFI is:

$$NPC_S \text{ fresh flows of funds} = \sum_{t=1}^{T} \delta_t^{t-0.5} \cdot [DG_t + PC_t + RG_t$$

$$+ A_t \cdot (m_t - c_t) + DX_t] \qquad (3.3)$$

$$= \sum_{t=1}^{T} \delta_t^{t-0.5} \cdot FF_t.$$

True profit accrues through each year. Society could withdraw true profit as it accrues, but, in the absence of precise knowledge of the timing of flows, it is assumed that society lets the DFI keep true profit. Hence, true profit is like an inflow back-to-back with an outflow, and the two flows cancel out of the $NPC_S$. The treatment here ignores taxes and dividends, but Schreiner (1997) adjusts the framework to handle them.

At the end of the time frame, it is assumed that society gets an inflow equal to the net worth then present in the DFI. Net worth at the end includes all outflows from society to the DFI up to time $T$ plus true profit. The flow is discounted by $\delta_T^T$ :

$$\text{NPC}_S \text{ end net worth} = \delta_T^T \cdot \{E_0 + \sum_{t=1}^{T} [DG_t + PC_t + RG_t$$

$$+ A_t \cdot (m_t - c_t) + DX_t + TP_t]\} \tag{3.4}$$

$$= \delta_T^T \cdot [E_0 + \sum_{t=1}^{T} (FF_t + TP_t)].$$

The $\text{NPC}_S$ adds the discounted outflows (equations 3.2 and 3.3) and subtracts the discounted inflows (equation 3.4):

$$\text{NPC}_S = \text{discounted outflows} - \text{discounted inflows}$$

$$= E_0 + \sum_{t=1}^{T} \delta_t^{t-0.5} \cdot FF_t - \delta_T^T \cdot [E_0 + \sum_{t=1}^{T} (FF_t + TP_t)] \tag{3.5}$$

$$= (1 - \delta_T^T) \cdot E_0 + \sum_{t=1}^{T} (\delta_t^{t-0.5} - \delta_T^T) \cdot FF_t - \delta_T^T \cdot \sum_{t=1}^{T} TP_t.$$

The $\text{NPC}_S$ of the flows of funds between society and a DFI from time 0 to time $T$ has three terms. The first term is the cost of funds put in at the start. For society at time 0, start equity is worth $E_0$ when entrusted to the DFI at time 0 but only $\delta_T^T \cdot E_0$ when it comes back at time $T$. The cost is the present value of funds when they are put in less their present value when they come back.

The second term is the cost of fresh funds $FF_t$ injected after the start of the time frame. Seen from time 0, these funds are worth $\delta_t^{t-0.5}$ when entrusted to the DFI but only $\delta_T^T$ when the DFI gives them back. The cost is the difference.

The third term is the cost (or the gain) of the true profit built up by the DFI. Society gets this inflow at the end of the time frame, so the discount factor is $\delta_T^T$. For most DFIs, the sum of true profit since birth is negative, and this decreases the inflow back to society. This means that—in real, nominal, and present-value terms—society gets back fewer dollars than it put in. Of course, the $\text{NPC}_S$—like the SDI—cannot account for social benefits or costs not reflected in the financial statements of the DFI.

## What Questions Does the Net Present Cost to Society Inform?

The $\text{NPC}_S$ informs two important social questions that involve long time frames. In the first, the $\text{NPC}_S$ informs the question of whether it improves social welfare to use public funds to start a new DFI from scratch, ignoring all costs and benefits borne by members of the target group. In the second, the $NPC_S$ informs the question of whether it improves social welfare to maintain public support for a DFI from now on, again ignoring all costs and benefits borne by members of the target group.

The $NPC_S$ is negative if the worth of the inflows to society exceeds the worth of the outflows. Thus, the concept of net present cost mirrors the concept of present value. If a DFI imposes no costs on nonclients, then a negative $NPC_S$ indicates that a DFI would be a good social investment because its return exceeds that of the marginal public project. This requires true profits so large that, even when discounted from the end of the time frame back to the start, they exceed the cost of the funds used by the DFI.

## Is There a Long-Term Analog to the Subsidy Dependence Index?

A long-term SDI ($SDI_L$) tells the percentage change in revenue from loans that would make the $NPC_S$ zero (Schreiner 1997). To derive this, first write true profit $TP_t$ as revenue from loans $LP_t \cdot i_t$ plus $OROE_t$, all other revenues less other expenses:

$$TP_t = LP_t \cdot i_t + OROE_t. \qquad (3.6)$$

Now set the $NPC_S$ (equation 3.5) equal to zero and solve for the $SDI_L$, the percentage change in revenue from loans that would make the $NPC_S$ zero:

$$0 = (1 - \delta_T^T) \cdot E_0 + \sum_{t=1}^{T} (\delta_t^{t-0.5} - \delta_T^T) \cdot FF_t - \delta_T^T \cdot \sum_{t=1}^{T} [LP_t \cdot i_t$$

$$\cdot (1 + SDI_L) + OROE_t]$$

$$(3.7)$$

$$SDI_L = \frac{(1 - \delta_T^T) \cdot E_0 + \sum_{t=1}^{T} (\delta_t^{t-0.5} - \delta_T^T) \cdot FF_t - \delta_T^T \cdot \sum_{t=1}^{T} TP_t}{\delta_T^T \cdot \sum_{t=1}^{T} LP_t \cdot i_t} = \frac{NPC_S}{\delta_T^T \cdot \sum_{t=1}^{T} LP_t \cdot i_t}.$$

With data since birth, the $SDI_L$ tells how far a public DFI has been from subsidy independence since birth. With projected data from now on, the $SDI_L$ predicts how far a DFI is expected to be from subsidy independence.

## Is Subsidy in the Subsidy Dependence Index Just the One-Year Case of Net Present Cost to Society?

If average equity includes true profit, then subsidy in the SDI (equation 2.15) is not just the one-year case of the $NPC_S$ (equation 3.5). If true profit is positive (negative), then subsidy in the SDI is less (more) than in the $NPC_S$ because the SDI does not discount the flow of true profit, implying less (more) subsidy (Schreiner 1997). The $NPC_S$ assumes that true profit comes at the end of the year, but the SDI assumes that true profit comes in the middle of the year.

For example, suppose a DFI starts a year with equity of 100. It posts a true profit of 10 by the end of the year, and it gets no more fresh funds in the year. In a one-year time frame and with $m$ set at 10 percent, the $NPC_S$ is 0 because true profit is just enough to compensate for the opportunity cost of public funds in net worth:

$$NPC_S = (1 - \delta_T^T) \cdot E_0 + \sum_{t=1}^{T} (\delta_t^{t-0.5} - \delta_T^T) \cdot FF_t - \delta_T^T \cdot \sum_{t=1}^{T} \cdot TP_t$$

$$= (1 - \delta_1) \cdot E_0 + (\delta_1^{1-0.5} - \delta_1) \cdot FF_1 - \delta_1 \cdot TP_1 \qquad (3.8)$$

$$= (1 - 0.9091) \cdot 100 + (0.9535 - 0.9091) \cdot 0 - 0.9091 \cdot 10$$

$$= 9.09 - 9.09 = 0 \, .$$

The measure of subsidy in the framework of the SDI is 0.5:

$$S = m \cdot E + A \cdot (m - c) + K - P$$
$$= 0.10 \cdot [(100 + 100 + 10)/2] + 0 + 0 - 10 \qquad (3.9)$$
$$= 10.5 - 10 = 0.5.$$

If the measure of average equity excludes true profit, then the SDI does equal zero, because equity remains unchanged during the year. In this case, the SDI is the same as the one-year $NPC_S$:

$$S = m \cdot E + A \cdot (m - c) + K - P,$$
$$= 0.10 \cdot [(100 + 100)/2] + 0 + 0 - 10 \qquad (3.10)$$
$$= 10 - 10 = 0.$$

### Is the Net Present Cost to Society Better Than the Subsidy Dependence Index?

Both the SDI and the $NPC_S$ work well in short time frames. In practice, many people understand ROE, and the measure of subsidy in the SDI can be transformed into a Subsidy-Adjusted ROE. The SDI is useful if the user wants a quick, crude estimate, if the time frame is short, if inflation is low, and if the user understands ROE but not the $NPC_S$. Both the SDI and the $SDI_L$ (which uses the $NPC_S$) can be seen as measures of matching grants provided to members of a target group through a DFI.

Unlike the SDI, the $NPC_S$ works in long time frames and is recognized as the best tool to judge projects (Brigham and Gapenski 1993). Choices may be sub-optimal investments if based on the SDI instead of on the $NPC_S$, especially in long time frames and in particular when an SDI that indicates subsidy independence takes place only after years of SDIs that indicate subsidy dependence.

## What Are the Net Present Cost to Society and the Subsidy Dependence Index in the Long Term for the Example Development Finance Institution?

For the example DFI, the $NPC_S$ and $SDI_L$ for three time frames that start at birth (the start of Year 00) are in table 3.1. The first time frame ends at the end of Year 01, the second at the end of Year 02, and the third at the end of Year 03. Table 3.1 also shows the one-year $NPC_S$ and the SDI based on the one-year $NPC_S$.

### Time Frame from Birth to the End of Year 01

With the opportunity cost of public funds to society $m_1$ set at 10 percent, the discount rate $\delta_1^1$ from the point of view of the birth of the DFI for a flow at the end of Year 01 is $1/(1 + 0.1) \doteq 0.9091$ (line Fc). The discount rate $\delta_1^{1-0.5}$ for flows in the middle of the year is $[1/(1 + 0.1)]^{0.5} \doteq 0.9535$ (line Fd). Start equity $E_0$ for the example DFI is 0 (line Fo). Direct grants $DG_1$ were 1,700 and paid-in capital $PC_1$ was 300. Revenue grants $RG_1$ were 400. The discount on public debt $A_1 \cdot (m_1 - c_1)$ was 10. Discounts on expenses $DX_1$ were 100. Total fresh funds $FF_1$ were $1,700 + 300 + 400 + 10 + 100 = 2,510$ (line Fj). True profit $TP_1$ was –310 (line Fn). The $NPC_S^{0-1}$ from the start to the end of Year 01 was:

$$NPC_S^{0-1} = (1 - \delta_1) \cdot E_0 + (\delta_1^{0.5} - \delta_1) \cdot FF_1 - \delta_1 \cdot TP_1$$
$$\doteq (1 - 0.9091) \cdot 0 + (0.9535 - 0.9091) \cdot 2,510 - 0.909 \cdot (-310) \quad (3.11)$$
$$\doteq 111.44 + 281.82 \doteq 393.28.$$

Subsidy in the SDI for Year 01 is 420 (line Cq of table 2.4). Because average equity includes true profit and because true profit is negative (the most common case), the SDI is more than the $NPC_S$.

Revenue from loans $LP_1 \cdot i_1$ is 420. The SDI for the example DFI in Year 01 is 1.00 (line Cx of table 2.4), but the $SDI_L^{0-1}$ is (line Fv of table 3.1):

$$SDI_L^{0-1} = \frac{NPC_S^{0-1}}{\delta_1 \cdot LP_1 \cdot i_1} = \frac{393.27}{0.9091 \cdot 420} \doteq 1.03. \quad (3.12)$$

**Table 3.1  Net Present Cost to Society**

| Line | | | 12/31/01 | 12/31/02 | 12/31/03 |
|---|---|---|---|---|---|
| **For one-year time frames** | | | | | |
| Fa | Disc. flow at end of year | $1/(1+Cd)$ | 0.9091 | 0.9091 | 0.9091 |
| Fb | Disc. flow middle of year | $[1/(1+Cd)]^{0.5}$ | 0.9535 | 0.9535 | 0.9535 |
| **For time frames that start at birth** | | | | | |
| Fc | Disc. flow at end of year | $Fc_{t-1}/(1+Cd)$ | 0.9091 | 0.8264 | 0.7513 |
| Fd | Disc. flow middle of year | $Fc_{t-1}\cdot[1/(1+Cd)]^{0.5}$ | 0.9535 | 0.8668 | 0.7880 |
| Fe | Change direct grants, $DG$ | Df | 1,700 | 300 | 300 |
| Ff | Change paid-in capital, $PC$ | Di | 300 | 345 | 265 |
| Fg | Revenue grants, $RG$ | Bl | 400 | 400 | 400 |
| Fh | Discount public debt, $A \cdot (m-c)$ | Cl | 10 | 30 | 50 |
| Fi | Discounts on expenses, $DX$ | Bn | 100 | 100 | 100 |
| Fj | Fresh funds in year, $FF$ | Fe + Ff + Fg + Fh + Fi | 2,510 | 1,175 | 1,115 |
| Fk | Accum. discounted fresh funds | $Fk_{t-1}$ + Fd · Fj | 2,393 | 3,412 | 4,290 |
| Fl | Accum. fresh funds | $Fl_{t-1}$ + Fj | 2,510 | 3,685 | 4,800 |
| Fm | True profits, $TP$ | Dn | (310) | (275) | 385 |
| Fn | Accum. true profit | $Fn_{t-1}$ + Fm | (310) | (585) | (200) |
| Fo | Start equity at birth, $E_0$ | $Ao_0$ | 0 | 0 | 0 |
| Fp | Start equity this year, $E_0$ | $Ao_{t-1}$ | 0 | 2,200 | 3,100 |
| Fq | One-year $NPC_S$ | $(1 - Fa) \cdot Fp + Fj \cdot (Fb - Fa) - Fm \cdot Fa$ | 393 | 502 | (19) |
| Fr | $NPC_S$ from birth | $(1 - Fc) \cdot Fo + Fk - Fc \cdot Fl - Fn \cdot Fc$ | 393 | 850 | 834 |
| Fs | Revenue from lending, $LP \cdot i$ | Ba | 420 | 1,080 | 1,700 |
| Ft | Accum. rev. from lending | $Ft_{t-1}$ + Fs | 420 | 1,500 | 3,200 |
| Fu | One-year SDI with $NPC_S$ | Fq/(Fa· Fs) | 1.03 | 0.51 | (0.01) |
| Fv | Long-run SDI | Fr/(Fc· Ft) | 1.03 | 0.69 | 0.35 |

*Note:* Monetary figures in constant units.
*Source:* Example of authors.

The DFI could have been privately profitable with 103 percent more revenue from loans. With the size of the loan portfolio held constant and with the actual yield at 0.40, this implies a change in yield of $0.40 \cdot 1.03 \doteq 0.41$ and a subsidy-free yield of $0.40 + 0.41 = 0.81$.

## Time Frame from Birth to the End of Year 02

With $m_2$ at 10 percent, the discount rate $\delta_2^2$ from birth to the end of Year 02 is $[1/(1 + 0.1)]^2 \doteq 0.8264$ (line Fc of table 3.1). The discount rate $\delta_2^{2-0.5}$ for flows in the middle of the year is $[1/(1 + 0.1)]^{1.5} \doteq 0.8668$ (line Fd). Direct grants $DG_2$ are 300, paid-in capital $PC_2$ is 345, revenue grants $RG_2$ are 400, the discount on public debt $A_2 \cdot (m_2 - c_2)$ is 30, and discounts on expenses $DX_2$ are 100. Total fresh funds $FF_2$ are $300 + 345 + 400 + 30 + 100 = 1,175$ (line Fj). True profit $TP_2$ was $-275$. Thus, the $NPC_S^{0-2}$ for the first two years of the example DFI was:

$$NPC_S^{0-2} = (1 - \delta_2^2) \cdot E_0 + \sum_{t=1}^{2} (\delta_t^{t-0.5} - \delta_2^2) \cdot FF_t - \delta_2^2 \cdot \sum_{t=1}^{T} TP_t$$

$$= (1 - 0.8264) \cdot 0$$
$$+ (0.9535 - 0.8264) \cdot 2{,}510 + (0.8668 - 0.8264) \qquad (3.13)$$
$$\cdot 1{,}175 - 0.8264 \cdot (-310 - 275)$$
$$\doteq 319.02 + 47.47 + 483.44 = 849.93.$$

Revenue from loans $LP_2 \cdot i_2$ is 1,080. The $SDI_L^{0-2}$ is:

$$SDI_L^{0-2} = \frac{NPC_S^{0-2}}{\delta_2^2 \sum_{t=1}^{2} LP_t \cdot i_t} = \frac{849.93}{0.8264 \cdot (420 + 1{,}080)} \doteq 0.69. \qquad (3.14)$$

## Time Frame from Birth to the End of Year 03

With $m_3$ at 10 percent, the discount rate $\delta_3^3$ from birth to the end of Year 03 is $[1/(1 + 0.1)]^3 \doteq 0.7513$ (line Fc of table 3.1). The discount rate $d_3^{3-0.5}$ for constant flows is $[1/(1 + 0.1)]^{2.5} \doteq 0.7880$. Direct grants $DG_3$ are 300, paid-in capital $PC_3$ is 265, revenue grants $RG_3$ are 400, the discount on public debt $A_3 \cdot (m_3 - c_3)$ is 50, and discounts on expenses $DX_3$ are 100. Total fresh funds $FF_3$ are $300 + 265 + 400 + 50 + 100 = 1,115$. True profit $TP_3$ is 385. The $NPC_S^{0-3}$ is:

$$\text{NPC}_S^{0-3} = (1 - \delta_3^3) \cdot E_0 + \sum_{t=1}^{3} (\delta_t^{t-0.5} - \delta_3^3) \cdot FF_t - \delta_3^3 \cdot \sum_{t=1}^{3} TP_t$$
$$= (1 - 0.7513) \cdot 0 + (0.9535 - 0.7513) \cdot 2{,}510$$
$$+ (0.8668 - 0.7513) \cdot 1{,}175 + (0.7880 - 0.7513) \tag{3.15}$$
$$\cdot 1{,}115 - 0.7513 \cdot (-310 - 275 + 385)$$
$$\doteq 507.52 + 135.71 + 40.92 + 150.26 = 834.41.$$

Revenue from loans $LP_3 \cdot i_3$ is 1,700. The $\text{SDI}_L^{0-3}$ is:

$$\text{SDI}_L^{0-3} = \frac{\text{NPC}_S^{0-3}}{\delta_3^3 \cdot \sum_{t=1}^{3} LP_t \cdot i_t} = \frac{834.41}{0.7513 \cdot (420 + 1{,}080 + 1{,}700)} \doteq 0.35. \tag{3.16}$$

The example DFI had an actual yield $i$ over the three-year time frame of 0.40. All else constant, an increase in the yield in each year of $0.40 \cdot 0.35 = 0.14$ would have led to subsidy independence. The subsidy-free yield for the lifetime of the DFI would be $0.40 + 0.14 = 0.54$. If the yield on loans $i$ had been 54 percent in all three years instead of 40 percent, then the $\text{NPC}_S$ for the three-year time frame would have been zero.

The example DFI was subsidy-independent in Year 03 (SDI of 0.00) even though it was not subsidy-independent from birth through Year 03 ($\text{SDI}_L$ of 0.35). Thus, measurement of the social cost of public DFIs should include both the short-term SDI and the long-term SDI. The two measures cannot be compared directly because the SDI uses undiscounted values and the $\text{SDI}_L$ uses discounted values.

# 4

# What Are the Pitfalls When Calculating the Subsidy Dependence Index or Net Present Cost to Society?

The use of the SDI and the $NPC_S$ in practice presents two key challenges. The first is the need to pick a meaningful social opportunity cost. The second is the need to cope with the constraints of accounting data within an economic framework.

## What Is the Social Opportunity Cost?

The *social opportunity cost* is defined as the return to public funds in the marginal public project. Because it is difficult to measure and a wide range of reasonably defensible estimates of social opportunity costs appear in the literature, chapter 1 discussed five proxies. Regardless of the proxy, the SDI and the $NPC_S$ are useful inasmuch as they show orders of magnitude and trends. When the proxy is lower than the true social opportunity cost, then the SDI and $NPC_S$ also are lower bounds on true social costs. Results in Schreiner (1997) suggest that long-term measures such as the $SDI_L$ are not very sensitive to the social opportunity cost because the vast bulk of cash flows take place long after the start of the time frame.

Two other important points about social opportunity costs from chapter 1 are repeated here. First, the social opportunity cost is not necessarily the cost to the DFI of public funds. Second, the social opportunity cost is not necessarily the opportunity cost of a private entity, that is, the cost to replace public funds with private funds. It is not uncommon to confuse social and private opportunity costs.

## What Can Be Done to Cope with Accounting Data?

The most important caveat for the SDI and $NPC_S$ is that they use accounting data that were not designed for economic (present-value) analysis. For example, accrued revenue in the income statement may never be collected. Even if the DFI eventually collects all accrued revenue or if it provides for all expected losses from unpaid accrued revenue, the financial statements still overstate the present value of accrued revenue. In general, items in the balance sheet are not recorded in terms of their present values; for example, debt and fixed assets are recorded at their cost to the DFI. The income statement of the DFI often does not distinguish between cash items and accrued items, nor does it distinguish between flows at different times within a reported period.

Of course, the SDI and the $NPC_S$ are limited by the data and assumptions fed to them. As in all financial analysis, good outputs require good inputs. This is not a weakness of the measures described here but rather a standard caveat of all analysis, especially when accounting data are stretched to fit economic purposes.

Like any disciplined attempt to measure performance, the SDI and the $NPC_S$ are like canaries in a coal mine that serve to unearth deviations from GAAP and International Accounting Standards. In this case, any financial indicator based on these weak data would probably be of low quality. Measurement helps to discover these weaknesses so that they can be addressed.

By far the two most important problems with the accounting data of DFIs are the failure to provide properly for loan losses and the failure to adjust for inflation. Either failure can result in financial statements that do not accurately reflect financial performance. When failures are substantial, any financial analysis is either meaningless or misleading.

## Why Should a Development Finance Institution Provide for Loan Losses?

Financial statements should reflect business performance. The business of DFIs is to produce financial services such as deposits and loans, and, in general, defaults and loan losses are a normal part of doing business. A loan may not turn sour for a long time, but a DFI should record the expected expense of the loss at disbursement. This conservatively reflects that some loans will go bad, even though, at disbursement, the DFI does not know which ones (Christen 1997). *Ex post* write-offs of bad loans understate profit in the year of the write-offs and overstate profits in past years.

Thus, a DFI should incur expenses for provision for loan losses constantly as it makes loans. These expenses build the reserve for loan losses, a contra-asset account. The *net loan portfolio* is the value of loans outstanding that the DFI expects to recover. It is the gross loan portfolio—which includes all loans outstanding, some of which will not be repaid—minus the reserve for loan losses.

If the DFI does not provide enough for loan losses, then it deflates expenses and inflates profits and net worth. The reserve for loan losses is too small, and the net portfolio is too big. Other authors discuss how to estimate the amount of provision for loan losses (Christen 1997; Von Pischke and others 1988; Bolnick 1988).

Often DFIs do not provide enough for loan losses. This distorts all financial ratios, including the SDI and the $NPC_S$. An important part of the business of a DFI is to make loans and to collect them, so any measure of performance must be based on financial statements that reflect the true risk of loans in the portfolio.

The example DFI did not provide for loan losses at all (line Bi of table 2.3). Most DFIs, however, cannot recover all their loans. Suppose that in each of the three years the DFI made 100 in loans that later turned bad. Thus, in each year the DFI should have incurred expenses of 100 as provision for loan losses. It is assumed that the DFI did not accrue revenue from interest. If it had, then the recognition of the bad loans would also require an adjustment to decrease accrued revenue from loans.

In the adjusted balance sheet, the reserve for loan losses changes by –100 each year (line Jc of table 4.1). The net portfolio (line Jd) and total assets (line Jg) shrink in step. Retained earnings (line Jn) fall because accounting profit falls.

The ripple effects of provision for loan losses are shaded in the adjusted income statement (table 4.2). The expense for loan-loss provisions increases from zero to 100 in each year (line Ki), and this changes the operating margin (line Kk) and accounting profit (line Km).

Adequate provision for loan losses also changes the SDI. Without adequate provision, the SDI was 1.00, 0.50, and 0.00 (line Cx of table 2.4). With adequate provision, the SDI is 1.18, 0.52, and –0.01 (line Gb of table 4.3). These are small differences, but the effects of proper provisions would be much larger for many DFIs.

Inadequate provision for loan losses leads to an inaccurate SDI and to inadequate financial ratios in general. Without provisions, ROE is 0.18, 0.10, and 0.24 (line En of table 2.6). With provisions, ROE falls to 0.10, 0.06, and 0.23 (line Ge of table 4.3). Provisions cause the SAROE to change from –0.28, –0.10, and 0.10 (line Eo of table 2.6) to –0.37, –0.13, and 0.11 (line Gf of table 4.3). ROA and SAROA follow the same pattern. Table 4.3 shows the SDI, the $NPC_S$, and the $SDI_L$ with provisions for loan losses. Yaron (1992b) provides more discussion of provisions for loan losses.

## Why Should a Development Finance Institution Adjust for the Effects of Inflation?

Inflation wreaks havoc with financial statements prepared under the assumption that monetary figures keep a constant value (Goldschmidt, Shashua, and Hillman 1986). Adjustments help to ensure that the data

**Table 4.1. Balance Sheet with Loan Losses**

| Line | | | 12/31/01 | 12/31/02 | 12/31/03 |
|------|---|---|---------|---------|---------|
| **Assets** | | | | | |
| Ja | Cash | Data | 600 | 700 | 800 |
| Jb | Loan portfolio (gross) | Data | 2,100 | 3,300 | 5,200 |
| Jc | Reserve for loan losses | Data | (100) | (100) | (100) |
| Jd | Loan portfolio (net) *LP* | Jb + Jc | 2,000 | 3,200 | 5,100 |
| Je | Investments, *I* | Data | 200 | 400 | 600 |
| Jf | Fixed assets (net) | Data | 100 | 200 | 200 |
| Jg | Total assets | Ja + Jd + Je + Jf | 2,900 | 4,500 | 6,700 |
| **Liabilities** | | | | | |
| Jh | Deposit liabilities | Data | 200 | 400 | 600 |
| Ji | Private debt | Data | 200 | 300 | 400 |
| Jj | Public debt, *A* | Data | 400 | 800 | 1,200 |
| Jk | Total liabilities | Jh + Ji + Jj | 800 | 1,500 | 2,200 |
| **Equity** | | | | | |
| Jl | Paid-in capital, *PC* | Data | 300 | 645 | 910 |
| Jm | Direct grants, *DG* | Data | 1,700 | 2,000 | 2,300 |
| Jn | Retained earnings | $Jn_{t-1}$ + Km | 100 | 255 | 1,090 |
| Jo | Total equity | Jl + Jm + Jn | 2,100 | 2,900 | 4,300 |
| Jp | Total equity and liabilities | Jk + Jo | 2,900 | 4,400 | 6,500 |

*Note:* Monetary figures in constant units.
*Source:* Example of authors.

65

**Table 4.2. Income Statement with Loan Losses**

| Line | | | 12/31/01 | 12/31/02 | 12/31/03 |
|------|---|---|---------|---------|---------|
| Ka | Revenue from loans, $LP \cdot i$ | Data | 420 | 1,080 | 1,700 |
| Kb | Revenue investments, $I \cdot j$ | Data | 5 | 15 | 25 |
| Kc | Total revenue from operations | $Ka + Kb$ | 425 | 1,095 | 1,725 |
| Kd | Expenses int. deposit liabilities | Data | 5 | 15 | 25 |
| Ke | Expenses int. private debt | Data | 10 | 25 | 35 |
| Kf | Expenses int. public debt, $A \cdot c$ | Data | 10 | 30 | 50 |
| Kg | Total int. exp. | $Kd + Ke + Kf$ | 25 | 70 | 110 |
| Kh | Financial margin | $Kc - Kg$ | 400 | 1,025 | 1,615 |
| Ki | Exp. prov. reserve for loan losses | Data | 100 | 100 | 100 |
| Kj | Exp. admin. | Data | 600 | 1,170 | 1,080 |
| Kk | Operating margin | $Kh - (Ki + Kj)$ | (300) | (245) | 435 |
| Kl | Revenue from grants, $RG$ | Data | 400 | 400 | 400 |
| Km | Accounting profit, $P$ | $Kk + Kl$ | 100 | 155 | 835 |

**Memo item:**

| | | | | | |
|------|---|---|---|---|---|
| Kn | Discounts on expenses, $DX$ | Data | 100 | 100 | 100 |

*Note*: Monetary figures in constant units.
*Source*: Example of authors.

**Table 4.3. Summary with Loan Losses**

| Line | | | 12/31/01 | 12/31/02 | 12/31/03 |
|------|---|---|---------|---------|---------|
| Ga | Subsidy, $S$ | Not shown | 495 | 565 | (25) |
| Gb | Subsidy Dependence Index, SDI | Not shown | 1.18 | 0.52 | (0.01) |
| Gc | ROA | Not shown | 0.07 | 0.04 | 0.15 |
| Gd | Subsidy-Adjusted ROA | Not shown | (0.27) | (0.09) | 0.07 |
| Ge | ROE | Not shown | 0.10 | 0.06 | 0.23 |
| Gf | Subsidy-Adjusted ROE | Not shown | (0.37) | (0.13) | 0.11 |
| Gg | One-year $NPC_S$ | Not shown | 465 | 527 | (41) |
| Gh | $NPC_S$ from birth | Not shown | 465 | 944 | 910 |
| Gi | One-year SDI with $NPC_S$ | Not shown | 1.22 | 0.54 | (0.03) |
| Gj | Long-run SDI | Not shown | 1.22 | 0.76 | 0.38 |

*Note:* Monetary figures in constant units. Average equity includes profit in current period.
*Source:* Example of authors.

measure what they intend to measure. Just as with provisions for loan losses, the problem is with the meaningfulness of the data, not with the measures that use the data.

IAS 29 suggests a few simple adjustments to use if the effects of inflation might affect the results of the analysis. The goal is a set of adjusted financial statements with the same meaning as unadjusted statements when prices are stable. Yaron (1992b) also discusses the need to adjust for inflation. Goldschmidt (1992) discusses IAS 29, and Goldschmidt and Yaron (1991) outline shortcut methods with numerical examples.

Christen (1997) adjusts for inflation (and for the effects of subsidized funds) directly and elegantly in the financial statements of an example DFI. Once adjusted, common financial measures such as ROE are meaningful.

The $NPC_S$ requires inflation-adjusted data unless inflation is zero for the whole time frame. Otherwise, monetary figures from different times are in different units and cannot be added together. Even if annual inflation is low, inflation adjustments are important in long time frames. If the SDI and $NPC_S$ are applied to inflation-adjusted figures, then opportunity costs should be in real terms because nominal rates with inflation-adjusted data would count costs twice (Yaron 1992b). The example DFI is assumed to be in an economy without inflation.

## What Are Other Pitfalls and Caveats?

### How Can Average Stocks Be Computed?

Given only year-end balance sheets, average stocks are half the sum of the start and end stocks. This monograph uses this method, but such two-point averages can mislead if actual cash flows are seasonal, lumpy, or otherwise nonuniform.

This is a data problem. Balance sheets are snapshots at a moment, and income statements sum revenues and expenses regardless of when they took place. A better average requires more frequent data from monthly or quarterly financial statements.

### Is Exemption from Reserve Requirements a Subsidy?

A deposit-taking DFI that is exempt from reserve requirements gets a subsidy (Benjamin 1994; Yaron 1992b). *Reserve requirements* are funds left on deposit with the central bank. They tax financial intermediation by reducing the return on deposits.

Exemption from reserve requirements lowers the cost to the DFI not only of deposits but also of equity and liabilities. Let $k$ be the reserve requirement, $\kappa$ the interest rate earned on required reserves (often zero), and $Dep$ the average deposit liability. The subsidy for a DFI exempt from reserve requirements is (Benjamin 1994; Yaron 1992b):

$$S = m \cdot E + A \cdot (m - c) + RG + DX - P$$
$$+ \frac{k \cdot [E \cdot (m - \kappa) + (A + Dep) \cdot (m - \kappa)]}{1 - k} \tag{4.1}$$

Without a reserve requirement, $k$ is zero, and the last term vanishes. Suppose that the example DFI is exempt from a reserve requirement $k$ of 20 percent and that required reserves earn no interest ($\kappa = 0$). Subsidy in Year 01 is then:

$$S = 0.1 \cdot 1{,}100 + 200 \cdot (0.1 - 0.05) + 400 + 100 - 200$$
$$+ \frac{0.2\,[1{,}100 \cdot (0.1 - 0) + (200 + 100) \cdot (0.01 - 0)]}{1 - 0.2} \tag{4.2}$$
$$= 110 + 10 + 300 + 0.2 \cdot (110 + 30)/0.8 = 420 + 35 = 455.$$

The SDI without the adjustment for the exemption from reserve requirements is $420/420 = 1.00$ (line Cx of table 2.4). With the exemption, the SDI is $455/420 \doteq 1.08$.

## How Can Exemption from Taxes on Profits Be Handled?

Most DFIs do not pay taxes on profits. This is a subsidy because a tax cut is like a cash gift. For simplicity, this monograph ignores taxes, but the frameworks of the SDI and the NPC$_S$ can be adjusted to handle taxes (Schreiner 1997).

## How Can Protection from Foreign Exchange Risk Be Handled?

Some DFIs hold debt denominated in foreign currencies but do not bear the risk that the exchange rate will change before payment is due. If a public entity absorbs the risk, then there is a subsidy defined as the difference in the payment with versus without protection, minus any premium paid by the DFI for insurance for exchange rate risk. One way to compute this—analogous to the discount on public debt as $A \cdot (m - c)$—is to assume that the DFI would replace foreign exchange with domestic currency ($A$) and then compute the subsidy per unit of foreign exchange as the price of equivalent domestic funds ($m$) minus the actual cost of foreign exchange ($c$).

## How Can Guarantees of Debt Be Handled?

Some DFIs have private debt backed by public guarantees. This debt is subsidized because the DFI would have to pay more for an equivalent unguaranteed loan. The subsidy is determined by the difference between the interest rate with and without the guarantee. Benjamin (1994, see appendix) provides a framework to estimate the cost of debt in the absence of guarantees.

## How Can Nonfinancial Services Be Handled?

DFIs often produce both financial and nonfinancial services (e.g., business training or agricultural extension). In most cases, each line of business should be analyzed by itself. Most of the work for the analyst is to divide the accounts, unless the DFI does it itself. Helms (1998), Christen (1997), and Yaron (1992b) discuss the issue and give example formats to help make the division. The fact that public funds are often earmarked for one line of business may help to simplify the division.

## How Can Apex Development Finance Institutions and Their First-Tier Customers Be Handled?

Apex DFIs make loans to first-tier DFIs that then re-lend to final borrowers (Gonzalez-Vega 1998). Care is required to make sure that all subsidies in the chain are counted once and only once. There are three basic guidelines.

First, although apex DFIs often charge the prime rate or some other "market" rate to DFIs, this rate is subsidized because it is still below the cost of funds from private sources. If public debt from the apex costs more than private debt, then the retail DFI would borrow on the market and skip the hassle of the apex DFI. The market price for a loan to a DFI is not the prime rate charged to blue-chip private firms but rather the price that covers all expected costs—including the cost of risk—of a loan to the DFI.

Second, the analyst must not double-count costs by adding social cost as seen at the level of the apex to social cost as seen at the level of the first-tier DFI. To see why not, suppose an apex DFI lends two dollars, one to each of two first-tier DFIs, and that the first-tier DFIs get no other funds from anywhere else in the year. If both first-tier DFIs go broke in one year, then society loses two dollars. The sum of the social cost of two dollars for the apex and the social cost of two dollars for the first-tier DFIs is four dollars, and society cannot lose more than it had loaned in the first place.

Third, it does not make sense to analyze only the apex or only the first-tier DFI. The whole system matters because the price charged by the apex is like an arbitrary transfer price between two subsidiaries with the same owner (society). The apex can set its price high or low to shuffle the revenues and expenses—and the measure of social cost—between the two tiers. Because public funds are used in both tiers, pricing policy should not affect the measure of social cost.

As an example, suppose an apex DFI has two identical first-tier customers, no debt, and 100 of paid-in capital from public sources through the year. The apex earns 6 per year on two loans of 50 to the first-tier DFIs at 6 percent interest. Because revenues are 6 and expenses are assumed to be zero, profit for the apex is 6. Given $K = 0$, $m = 0.1$, and $A = 0$, subsidy is $0.1 \cdot [(100 + 100 + 6)/2] + 0 \cdot (0.1 - 0) + 0 - 6 = 4.3$ (equation 2.10). The SDI is $4.3/6 \doteq 0.72$ (equation 2.7).

Now suppose that each of the first-tier DFIs has no expenses except for the 3 paid for their apex debt. Each first-tier DFI has 100 of paid-in capital from public sources through the year. With 50 of debt and 100 of net worth, each DFI gets revenue of 1 by lending 150 at an interest rate of two-thirds percent. Each posts a net return of $1 - 3 = -2$. Given that $K = 0$, $m = 0.1$, and $A = 50$, subsidy for each first-tier DFI is $0.1 \cdot [(100 + 100 - 2)/2] + 50 \cdot (0.1 - 0.03) + 0 - (-2) = 9.9 + 3.5 + 2 = 15.4$. The SDI is $15.4/1 = 15.4$.

The sum of the three measures of subsidy is $4.3 + 15.4 \cdot 2 = 35.1$. Because the revenue from loans to final borrowers is 2, the SDI for the system would be $35.1/2 = 17.55$. But this subsidy is not the social cost of the system, nor is this SDI the change in revenue from loans needed to make social cost equal to zero.

To see why, suppose that nothing changes except that the apex decreases its interest rate to 1 percent. Its profit falls to 1, and subsidy is $0.1 \cdot [(100 + 100 + 1)/2] + 0 \cdot (0.1 - 0) + 0 - 1 = 9.05$. For the first-tier DFIs, profit increases to $1 - 0.5 = 0.5$, and subsidy $S$ is $0.1 \cdot [(100 + 100 + 0.5)/2] + 50 \cdot (0.1 - 0.01) + 0 - 0.5 = 10.025 + 4.5 - 0.5 = 14.025$. The sum of the three measures of subsidy has changed to $9.05 + 14.025 \cdot 2 = 37.1$, and the SDI is now $37.1/2 = 18.55$.

By now the problem is clear. In both cases, all the DFIs were owned by society, $150 \cdot 2 = 300$ was lent to final borrowers, and revenue from loans to final borrowers was 2. Nothing changed except the transfer price between the DFIs, yet the supposed measure of social cost changed from 35.1 to 37.1.

The correct approach is to consolidate the financial statements of all DFIs in the system and then to compute subsidy. This removes the dependence on the transfer price (Stickney and Weil 1994). In this example, consolidated net worth is 300, the sum of net worth in each DFI. The debt liabilities of the first-tier DFIs cancel with the loan assets of the apex. This leaves 300 in consolidated assets as loans to final borrowers. Expenses are zero, revenues from loans are 2, and profit is $2 - 0 = 2$. Subsidy is $0.1 \cdot [(300 + 300 + 2)/2] + 0 \cdot (0.1 - 0.01) + 0 - 2 = 28.1$, and the system SDI is $28.1/2 = 14.05$.

## How Can Compensating Balances Be Handled?

Some loan contracts require borrowers to maintain a minimum deposit with the DFI until the loan is repaid. This decreases the effective loan portfolio $LP$. For example, a DFI with 100 in loans as assets and 10 in compensating balances as liabilities would have an effective loan portfolio not of 100 but of 90. Compensating balances are not subsidies because the (private) borrower accepts them as part of the price of the loan (IADB 1994). No public funds flow.

All else constant, the smaller effective loan portfolio $LP$ due to compensating balances does not affect the SDI nor the $NPC_S$ because it does not affect the revenues, expenses, or net worth of the DFI. It does, however, increase the yield on loans and thus increase the subsidy-free yield; revenue from loans $LP \cdot i$ is unchanged, but the effective loan portfolio $LP$ decreases, so the yield on loans $i$ must increase.

Suppose that all the deposit liabilities of the example DFI (line Ah in table 2.2) are compensating balances. The average loan portfolio $LP$ decreases from $(0 + 2,100)/2 = 1,050$ (line Ct of table 2.4) to $(0 + 2,100 - 200)/2 = 950$. Revenue from loans stays at 420 (line Ba of table 2.3). The yield on loans $i$, however, increases from $420/1,050 = 0.40$ to $420/950 \doteq 0.4421$ (equation 2.9). The SDI stays at 1.00 because neither $LP$ nor $i$ appear in it except through revenue from loans $LP \cdot i$, unchanged at $950 \cdot 0.4421 \doteq 420$. The increase in $i$, however, increases the subsidy-free yield from 0.80 (line Caa of table 2.4) to $0.44 \cdot (1 + 1.00) = 0.88$ (equation 2.17).

## Does It Make Sense to Regress the Subsidy Dependence Index on Items from the Financial Statements?

It does not make sense to regress the SDI against items from the financial statements. Regressions assume a stochastic relationship between dependent and independent variables, but the SDI has an exact, known relationship to all items in the financial statements. This requires not statistics but algebra.

In contrast, it may make sense to regress the SDI on factors not in its formula. For example, Benjamin (1994) regressed the SDI on the age of a nonrandom sample of microfinance DFIs. He found that the SDI decreased with age.

## What Are the Key Caveats?

The SDI and the NPC$_S$ are subject to six often-misunderstood caveats.

- The SDI does not say that all DFIs should raise interest rates until subsidy is zero.
- Neither the SDI nor the NPC$_S$ pretends to answer all questions asked about financial performance from all points of view. Standard financial analysis is still useful as long as it uses meaningful data.
- Comprehensive analyses should consider not only the SDI itself but also the level of subsidy, the actual yield, the subsidy-free yield, and the absolute change in the yield that would make subsidy zero.
- Neither the SDI nor the NPC$_S$ pretends to measure benefits.
- The SDI and the NPC$_S$ require the analyst to find meaningful data and opportunity costs and to use the results to suggest ways to improve performance.
- The SDI measures subsidy dependence as seen by society, not private profitability as seen by a private entity.

The SDI and the NPC$_S$ are useful as measures of the social cost of DFIs and thus as part of the process that allots public funds. They are useful even in the absence of measures of benefits, although the existence of measures of cost should not be used to advocate for the irrelevance of benefits. An example is the issue of agricultural extension, often provided free to clients by agricultural DFIs. It is expensive to measure the benefits of extension. In contrast, it is inexpensive to measure the costs. Once costs are known, the pursuit of efficiency and improved social welfare can focus on down-to-earth questions. Is there a new technology that needs extension to speed its spread? Could farmers pay for it? Should only rich farmers be asked to pay for it? Should fees be phased in? Would subcontractors cost less and provide better service than the employees of the DFI?

# 5
# Recent Proposed Changes to the Subsidy Dependence Index

The importance of the social cost of DFIs has prompted several attempts to refine the SDI or to use other standards to judge performance. This chapter presents critiques of three recent proposals. They fix what is not broken, or they tweak the SDI to answer unimportant questions. This chapter is based on Schreiner and Yaron (1999).

## The Subsidy Dependence Ratio of Khandker

In several papers on DFIs in Bangladesh, Khandker proposes the Subsidy Dependence Ratio (SDR) as an alternative to the SDI (Khandker and Khalily 1996; Khandker, Khalily, and Khan 1995). Similar measures have also been proposed by Holtmann and Mommartz (1996), SEEP (1995), and the IADB (1994).

These authors are concerned that the SDI compares subsidy only with revenue from loans even though DFIs also get revenue from investments in nonloan assets such as treasury bills. In principle, a DFI could decrease its subsidy dependence through increased revenues either from loans or from investments.

The SDR compares subsidy with revenue both from loans and from investments. Fixing the fact that the SDR of Khandker, Khalily, and Khan omits $K$, if $j$ is the yield on investments and if $I$ is the average investment so $I \cdot j$ is revenue from investments, then the SDR is:

$$\text{SDR} = \frac{S}{LP \cdot i + I \cdot j}. \tag{5.1}$$

Both the SDR and the SDI have subsidy $S$ in the numerator. Like the SDI, the SDR is negative if and only if an SAROE exceeds the social opportunity cost. Thus, the SDR and the SDI do not differ in their most important aspect, the measurement of subsidy. They differ only in what they compare with subsidy.

## What Question Does the Subsidy Dependence Ratio Answer?

The SDR tells how much more revenue from loans and investments would be needed to reach subsidy independence. This is not a very useful question. While most DFIs have some degree of local monopoly and some freedom to set the price of their loans, DFIs are probably price takers in the investment market. If a DFI could get a higher rate of return on investments without more risk, then presumably it would have already done so (IADB 1994). More importantly, the mission of a DFI is not to invest in nonloan assets but to make loans to members of a target group.

In general, it is true that a DFI can decrease social cost via any increased revenue or decreased expense, so it is indeed useful to compare subsidy not only with revenue from loans but also with other revenue and expense items. But the biggest, most malleable item is revenue from loans, and lending is the main purpose of a DFI. DFIs do invest in order to maintain liquidity and to meet demand from clients for loans and withdrawals of deposits, but investment is not their main line of business.

The numerator of both the SDR and the SDI is subsidy. The denominator of the SDI is revenue from loans, while the denominator of the SDR is revenue from loans and from investments. Thus, the SDR is always less than or equal to the SDI. In almost all cases, the need to maintain liquidity means that investments are nonzero, and so the SDR makes a DFI look less subsidy-dependent than the SDI. If investments are large compared with loans—as is the case in some years for some of the DFIs studied by Khandker—then the SDR is much smaller than the SDI. This misleads because a DFI cannot increase the rate of return on its investments at will unless it also assumes more risk and because the purpose of DFIs is to make loans to the target group. (An SDR of 100 percent implies that a DFI could become subsidy-independent by doubling the yield on both loans and investments. Even if the DFI could double the yield on loans, however, it could not double the yield on investments without incurring much more risk. Thus, the elimination of subsidy would imply more than a doubling of the yield on loans, suggesting that the SDR understates subsidy and overstates subsidy independence.)

For example, the SDR gives an unfair assessment of Grameen Bank, the best-known DFI in the world (Yaron, Benjamin, and Piprek 1997, p. 146):

[The SDR] results in an understatement of Grameen's dependence on subsidies, particularly during its initial years of operation, when a larger share of its financial resources was invested in the capital market. The measure therefore also underestimates the subsequent progress Grameen made in reducing its dependence on subsidies as the share of funds invested in the capital market declined relative to the share of funds loaned to clients. Following [the logic of the SDR], a microfinance institution could appear increasingly independent of subsidies simply by reducing its loans outstanding.

## How Is the Subsidy Dependence Ratio Motivated?

Khandker, Khalily, and Khan justify the SDR as follows (1995, p. 46):

As part of a prudent risk-reducing policy, a financial institution may diversify its financial resources to maximize expected return and profit. This needs to be taken into account while calculating the SDI. Otherwise, even if everything else remains the same, a portfolio mix can yield a higher profit for a program that diversifies resources compared to a program that only lends, and consequently, [the] SDI differs by program.

While more loans may indeed mean more losses if the rush to make more loans leads to more default, the above claim is weak on two counts. First, the variance of the SDI across DFIs is not a weakness but a strength. A measure that did not vary would be useless. Second, the SDI does account for the diversification of assets because the measure of subsidy in the numerator includes profit and thus, by definition, all revenue from all sources, including investments.

Khandker, Khalily, and Khan also offer a second motivation of the SDR (1995, p. 47):

To the extent that a program always minimizes its income risk through portfolio diversification, the SDR appears more consistent than the SDI with such a practice, and consequently is subject to less variation over time and across programs.

We disagree with this claim on two counts. First, few DFIs minimize income risk. Indeed, Khandker, Khalily, and Khan (1995) suggest that DFIs "maximize expected return and profit" (p. 46), which would require anything but to minimize risk. Second, variation in how funds are split between investment and lending over time and across programs has the same effect on the numerator of both the SDR and the SDI. The fact that the denominator of the SDR is always greater than or equal to the denominator of the SDI means that the SDR will be less than or equal to the SDI.

While this does indeed imply that the SDR has less variation than the SDI, the reduced sensitivity also means that the SDR dampens differences and so is less useful as a tool to assess performance.

Finally, Khandker, Khalily, and Khan (1995) claim that the SDI prescribes higher yields on loans as the only way to reduce subsidy dependence. This is not true (Yaron 1992a, 1992b). Increased yields on loans may indeed often be the easiest, quickest, and most practical way to decrease subsidy dependence, but a DFI that pursues efficiency will also use economies of scale, high recuperation, decreases in operating costs, and increases in deposit mobilization. For the example DFI and for the sample of DFIs in Benjamin (1994), subsidy independence resulted not so much from increased interest rates as from improved efficiency with age and growth.

## What Is the Subsidy Dependence Ratio for the Example Development Finance Institution?

The SDR has the same numerator as the SDI but a bigger denominator:

$$
\begin{aligned}
\mathrm{SDR}_{01} &= \frac{m \cdot E + A \cdot (m - c) + K - P}{LP \cdot i + I \cdot j} \\
&= \frac{0.10 \cdot 1{,}100 + 200 \cdot (0.10 - 0.05) + 500 - 200}{1{,}050 \cdot 0.40 + 100 \cdot 0.05} \\
&= 420/425 \doteq 0.988.
\end{aligned}
\tag{5.2}
$$

The SDI was $420/420 = 1.00$ (line Cx of table 2.4), saying that the example DFI could be subsidy-independent if the yield on loans increased by 100 percent. In contrast, the SDR says that the example DFI could be subsidy-independent if the yields both on loans and on investments increased by 99 percent. Most DFIs are price makers for their loans to their specific target groups and price takers for their investments. Thus, a DFI could probably increase the yield on loans but not the yield on investments.

To see the weakness of the SDR, suppose that the example DFI got an extra direct grant $DG$ of 1,000 at the start of Year 01 and invested it at a yield $j$ of 5 percent. If the new direct grant does not increase expenses, then accounting profits grow by $1{,}000 \cdot 0.05 = 50$. Average equity grows by 1,025, the 1,000 granted at the start of the year plus half of 50, the extra profit from the investment in the year. The DFI used more public funds but did not produce any more loans to the target group. The SDI reflects this downturn in performance because it increases by 0.13, from 1.00 to 1.13:

$$\text{SDI}_{01}' = \frac{m \cdot E + A \cdot (m - c) + K - P}{LP \cdot i}$$

$$= \frac{0.10 \cdot (1{,}100 + 1{,}025) + 200 \cdot (0.10 - 0.05) + 500 - (200 + 50)}{1{,}050 \cdot 0.40} \quad (5.3)$$

$$= 472.5/420 \doteq 1.13.$$

The SDR, in contrast, increases only 0.007, from 0.988 to 0.995:

$$\text{SDI}_{01}' = \frac{m \cdot E + A \cdot (m - c) + K - P}{LP \cdot i + I \cdot j}$$

$$= \frac{0.10 \cdot (1{,}100 + 1{,}025) + 200 \cdot (0.10 - 0.05) + 500 - (200 + 50)}{1{,}050 \cdot 0.40 + (100 + 1{,}000) \cdot 0.05} \quad (5.4)$$

$$= 472.5/475 \doteq 0.995.$$

Social cost increased from 420 to 472.5, and the DFI produced the same loans to the target group. How did the performance of the DFI change? The SDI suggests that it worsened a lot. In contrast, the SDR suggests that it barely changed.

If $(m - j)/j < \text{SDR}$, then investments of extra direct grants will decrease the SDR even though the SDI increases. In the example above, $m = 0.10$, $j = 0.05$, and investment of extra direct grants increased the SDR slightly because $(0.10 - 0.05)/0.05 = 1 > \text{SDR} \doteq 0.988$. Usually, however, $(m - j)/j < \text{SDR}$. For example, if the return on investments $j$ increased from 0.05 to 0.06, then $(0.10 - 0.06)/0.06 \doteq 0.667 < \text{SDR} \doteq .988$. Investment of extra direct grants still increases the SDI, from 1.00 to 1.10:

$$\text{SDI}_{01}'' = \frac{m \cdot E + A \cdot (m - c) + K - P}{LP \cdot i}$$

$$= \frac{0.10 \cdot (1{,}100 + 1{,}030) + 200 \cdot (0.10 - 0.05) + 500 - (200 + 60)}{1{,}050 \cdot 0.40} \quad (5.5)$$

$$= 463/420 \doteq 1.10.$$

The SDR, however, *decreases*, from 0.988 to 0.953:

$$\text{SDI}_{01}'' = \frac{m \cdot E + A \cdot (m - c) + K - P}{LP \cdot i + I \cdot j}$$

$$= \frac{0.10 \cdot (1{,}100 + 1{,}030) + 200 \cdot (0.10 - 0.05) + 500 - (200 + 60)}{1{,}050 \cdot 0.40 + (100 + 1{,}000) \cdot 0.06} \quad (5.6)$$

$$= 463/486 \doteq 0.953.$$

Investment of extra public funds increased social cost from 420 to 463. The SDI increased to reflect this, but the SDR decreased, suggesting that subsidy dependence decreased even though more public resources were used to produce the same output for the target group. Hence, the SDR is not a useful measure of subsidy dependence.

## The Profitability Gap of Sacay

Three concerns prompted Sacay (1996) to propose the Profitability Gap (PG) as an alternative to the SDI. First, Sacay wanted to compare subsidy with equity. Second, Sacay wanted to account for the subsidies implicit when a government allows a DFI to fall below minimum legal standards for capital adequacy. Third, Sacay said that the SDI assumes that subsidy can be decreased only by increases in the yield on loans.

These concerns are unfounded (Belli 1996b). First, a function of the measure of subsidy in the SDI is already equivalent to an SAROE. Second, most DFIs meet legal capital requirements. For those DFIs that do not, the PG proposed by Sacay counts some subsidies twice. Third, the SDI does not claim that the only way to remove subsidy is to increase the yield on loans.

### What Question Does the Profitability Gap of Sacay Answer?

The PG tells how far from a target SAROE is a DFI that gets subsidies from an exemption from legal capital standards, but this is not a very useful question. Given a target SAROE of $m$, the PG of Sacay is:

$$PG = m - \frac{P - A \cdot (m - c) - \max (0, E^{min} - E)}{E + \max (0, E^{min} - E)} \tag{5.7}$$

where $E^{min}$ is the minimum equity required by law and

$$\max (0, E^{min} - E) = \begin{cases} 0 \text{ if } 0 \geq E^{min} - E \\ E^{min} - E \text{ if } E^{min} - E > 0. \end{cases}$$

Sacay calls $\max (0, E^{min} - E)$ the *capital deficiency*. If capital exceeds the legal minimum, then the deficiency is zero. Otherwise, it is the minimum less actual equity.

With no capital deficiency, $E^{min} - E \leq 0$ and so $\max (0, E^{min} - E) = 0$. The PG is then:

$$PG_{\text{no deficiency}} = m - \frac{P - A \cdot (m - c) - 0}{E + 0}$$

$$= \frac{E \cdot m + A \cdot (m - c) - P}{E}. \tag{5.8}$$

The numerator of the PG with no capital deficiency, except for the lack of $K$, is the same as subsidy in the SDI. Without $K$, donors could force the PG as low as they like with profit grants. We adjust the PG to prevent this:

$$PG'_{\text{no deficiency}} = \frac{E \cdot m + A \cdot (m - c) + K - P}{E} = \frac{S}{E}. \tag{5.9}$$

With no capital deficiency, the PG compares subsidy with equity rather than with revenue from loans. Like the SDI, the PG is negative if and only if a Subsidy-Adjusted ROE exceeds the opportunity cost $m$:

$$PG \le 0 \Leftrightarrow \frac{m \cdot E - TP}{E} \le 0 \Leftrightarrow m \cdot E - TP \le 0 \Leftrightarrow m \cdot E \le TP \Leftrightarrow m \le \frac{TP}{E}. \tag{5.10}$$

For a capital-deficient DFI, the $PG$ proposed by Sacay (with $K$ added) is:

$$PG'_{\text{deficiency Sacay}} = m - \frac{P - A \cdot (m - c) - K - (E^{\min} - E)}{E + (E^{\min} - E)}$$

$$= \frac{E^{\min} \cdot m + A \cdot (m - c) + K - [P - (E^{\min} - E)]}{E^{\min}}. \tag{5.11}$$

The PG proposed by Sacay would adjust capital up to its legal minimum, taking the needed capital from profit and making it unavailable to compensate for subsidies. While it does make sense to charge an opportunity cost $m$ against the full minimum capital requirement $E^{\min}$, it does not make sense to take $E^{\min} - E$ from profit $P$. This would impute a social cost of $1 + m$ for each dollar of capital deficiency, $m$ for the use of the dollar for the year, and 1 because the dollar was used up. But the dollar was not used up, so the correct PG with capital deficiency should replace $E$ with $E^{\min}$ but not take the difference from profit:

$$PG'_{\text{deficiency}} = \frac{E^{\min} \cdot m + A \cdot (m - c) + K - P}{E^{\min}}. \tag{5.12}$$

None of the six example DFIs in Sacay (1996) had capital deficiencies. Whether the level of capital is adequate or deficient, the social opportunity cost of funds used by a DFI should be adjusted to reflect the risk due to its leverage (Benjamin 1994).

### Decreased Subsidy Dependence through an Increased Yield on Loans

The SDI does not assume that an increased yield on loans is the only way to decrease subsidy dependence. Among a host of factors, the SDI depends on loan recuperation, deposit mobilization, and administrative costs. The classic statement of the SDI repeatedly insists that a DFI can decrease its subsidy dependence in many ways (Yaron 1992b, pp. 5, 7, 23).

## The Average Subsidy Dependence Index of Hulme and Mosley

Two important works compute four-year averages of SDIs for 10 DFIs around the world (Mosley and Hulme 1998; Hulme and Mosley 1996, p. 44). The broad conclusions of these works depend on the average SDIs because they help to determine which DFIs are analyzed as ones with a focus on growth and sustainability.

The average SDI of Hulme and Mosley has two problems. First, it cannot be interpreted as the percentage increase in revenue on loans that would make subsidy zero. Second, its formula in the one-year case does not seem meaningful.

### The Ratio of Averages and the Average of Ratios

The ratio of averages is not the same as the average of ratios:

$$\frac{\left(\dfrac{a+b}{2}\right)}{\left(\dfrac{c+d}{2}\right)} \uparrow \frac{\left(\dfrac{a}{c}+\dfrac{b}{d}\right)}{2}. \tag{5.13}$$

The SDI is a ratio. Hulme and Mosley computed the average SDI as the average of ratios, the right-hand side of equation 5.13. But only the ratio of averages—the left-hand side of equation 5.13—keeps the meaning of the SDI as the percentage increase in lending that, all else constant, would make the sum of subsidy through the years zero.

For the first two years of the example DFI, the average SDI computed as the average of ratios (right-hand side of equation 5.13) is:

$$\frac{\left(\dfrac{a}{c}+\dfrac{b}{d}\right)}{2}=\frac{\left(\dfrac{S_1}{LP_1\cdot i_1}+\dfrac{S_2}{LP_2\cdot i_2}\right)}{2}=\frac{\left(\dfrac{420}{420}+\dfrac{540}{1{,}080}\right)}{2}=0.75. \quad (5.14)$$

A 75 percent increase in the yield on loans would increase profit in the first year by $0.75 \cdot 420 = 315$. Using start equity $E_0$ and not average equity $E$, this leaves a subsidy of $420 - 315 = 105$. In the second year, profits would increase by $0.75 \cdot 1{,}080 = 810$. This leaves a subsidy of $540 - 810 = -270$. The sum of subsidy in the two years is not zero but $105 - 270 = -165$.

In contrast, the ratio of averages (left-hand side of equation 5.13) is:

$$\frac{\left(\dfrac{a+b}{2}\right)}{\left(\dfrac{c+d}{2}\right)}=\frac{S_1+S_2}{LP_1\cdot i_1+LP_2\cdot i_2}=\frac{420+540}{420+1{,}080}=0.64. \quad (5.15)$$

A 64 percent increase in the yield on loans would increase profit in the first year by $0.64 \cdot 420 = 268.8$. Using start equity $E_0$ and not average equity $E$, this leaves a subsidy of $420 - 268.8 = 151.2$. In the second year, profits would increase by $0.64 \cdot 1{,}080 = 691.2$. This leaves a subsidy of $540 - 691.2 = -151.2$. The sum of subsidy in the two years is now zero.

In any case, the SDI should not be averaged across years because it is meaningful only in short time frames. In long time frames, a full picture of subsidy dependence requires a measure that discounts flows by when they take place (Schreiner 1997). If, as in Hulme and Mosley, the SDI is averaged through a long time frame anyway, then the analyst should divide the sum of subsidy in all years by the sum of revenue from loans in all years. This would preserve the interpretation of the SDI.

## The Loan Portfolio LP as a Proxy for Average Public Debt A

Public debt $A$ is a liability of a DFI, and the loan portfolio $LP$ is an asset. In general, the two are not equal. In fact, they differ markedly when the DFI mobilizes savings or when the DFI has a high ratio of equity to assets. Hulme and Mosley (1996, p. 92), however, replace $A$ with $LP$ in their measure of subsidy dependence. They also change the expression $(m - c)$ in the discount on public debt to $(c - m)$:

$$\text{Subsidy in Hulme and Mosley} = \frac{m \cdot E + LP \cdot (c - m) + K - P}{LP \cdot i}. \quad (5.16)$$

The formula in Hulme and Mosley (1996) follows neither the spirit nor the letter of the SDI. In private correspondence, Hulme and Mosley state that they deliberately replaced $A$ with $LP$, but they do not say whether the switch of $c$ and $m$ (which makes the discount on public debt negative) is a typographical error. The replacement of $A$ with $LP$ does not make sense because the social opportunity cost applies to the public funds used by a DFI, not to the funds loaned to the target group. Otherwise, a DFI that did not lend would have less subsidy than one that did. In later work (1998, p. 789), Hulme and Mosley write out the standard SDI formula, although they do not elaborate on the shift in the tool used to measure subsidy in DFIs.

# Appendix
# A Framework to Approximate the Opportunity Costs of Private Entities

This appendix presents a framework to approximate the opportunity costs of debt and equity for private entities. It is based on Benjamin (1994).

## What Is the Price of Private Debt?

The price of private debt depends on what kind of debt it is. The two options are deposits and market debt.

### When Will Deposits Replace Public Debt?

If a DFI takes deposits, it is assumed that deposits will replace public debt. The base cost is taken as the rate the DFI pays on deposits plus a mark-up of three percentage points (Benjamin 1994; Yaron 1992b). This assumes that a DFI could attract more deposits at the same rate it pays now. In practice, the assumed mark-up for administrative costs would be based on actual expected costs.

The example DFI paid 5 percent on deposits (line He of table A.1). With the mark-up, private deposits would cost 8 percent (line Hg).

### When Will Market Debt Replace Public Debt?

If a DFI does not take deposits, then it is assumed that private debt replaces public debt. The cost of private debt is taken as the local prime rate plus a premium for risk. Most DFIs are far riskier than blue-chip, prime-rate borrowers. In the example, the prime rate is 9 percent (line Hh of table A.1).

In some cases, a DFI that lost public support might replace some equity with private debt. But most DFIs are too weak to borrow on the market even with equity propped up by subsidized funds. Furthermore, lenders are unlikely to adjust interest rates more than a few percentage points to compensate for extra risk. Thus, most DFIs would not replace public equity with private debt.

**Table A.1. Private Opportunity Costs**

| Line | | | 12/31/01 | 12/31/02 | 12/31/03 |
|---|---|---|---|---|---|
| Ha | Start deposit liabilities | $Ah_{t-1}$ | 0 | 200 | 400 |
| Hb | End deposit liabilities | Ah | 200 | 400 | 600 |
| Hc | Average deposit liabilities, $Dep$ | (Ha + Hb)/2 | 100 | 300 | 500 |
| Hd | Exp. int. deposit liabilities | Bd | 5 | 15 | 25 |
| He | Rate paid deposit liabilities, $d$ | Hd/Hc | 0.05 | 0.05 | 0.05 |
| Hf | Adj. for extra administrative costs | Data | 0.03 | 0.03 | 0.03 |
| Hg | Opportunity cost public debt for deposits, $M$ | He + Hf | 0.08 | 0.08 | 0.08 |
| Hh | Prime rate | Data | 0.09 | 0.09 | 0.09 |
| Hi | Age of DFI in years | Data | 1 | 2 | 3 |
| Hj | Premium for age | 2/100/Hi | 0.02 | 0.010 | 0.007 |
| Hk | ROE | En | 0.18 | 0.10 | 0.24 |
| Hl | Premium for profitability | See text | 0.00 | 0.01 | 0.00 |
| Hm | Opportunity cost, debt for debt, $m$ | Hh + Hj + Hl | 0.11 | 0.11 | 0.10 |
| Hn | Start total liabilities | $Ak_{t-1}$ | 0 | 800 | 1,500 |
| Ho | End total liabilities | Ak | 800 | 1,500 | 2,200 |
| Hp | Average total liabilities | (Hn + Ho)/2 | 400 | 1,150 | 1,850 |
| Hq | Average equity, $E$ | Cc | 1,100 | 2,650 | 3,850 |
| Hr | Leverage, $L$ | Hp/Hq | 0.36 | 0.43 | 0.48 |
| Hs | Opportunity cost of equity, $M$ | Hm · (1.1 + 0.1 · Hr) | 0.13 | 0.13 | 0.11 |

*Note:* Monetary figures in constant units. Average equity includes profit in current period.
*Source:* Example of the authors based on Benjamin (1994).

HOW DOES EXPERIENCE AFFECT THE PRICE OF PRIVATE DEBT? Less-experienced DFIs pay more for private debt. Benjamin (1994) assumes that the experience premium to be added to the prime rate is $2/100/n$, where $n$ is the age of the DFI in years. All else constant, young DFIs are riskier than old DFIs because lenders do not know them as well and because they are more likely to go bankrupt. The example DFI adds 0.02 in the first year, 0.01 in the second year, and about 0.007 in the third year (line Hj of table A.1).

As with the mark-up for administrative costs to handle extra deposits, this crude assumption is meant to capture the spirit of risk premia for experience. In most cases, these numbers will provide a consistent base for comparison. In some cases, however, the analyst can pick risk premia matched to a specific DFI.

HOW DOES PROFITABILITY AFFECT THE PRICE OF PRIVATE DEBT? Profitable DFIs pay less for private debt because they are less risky. Benjamin (1994) illustrates this with a rule: If the DFI has an ROE of less than zero, then add 0.03 to the prime rate. If ROE is more than zero but less than the prime rate, then add 0.02. If ROE is more than the prime rate but less than twice the prime rate, then add 0.01. Otherwise, add nothing.

For the example DFI, the adjustment for profitability is zero in Years 01 and 03 (line Hl of table A.1). In Year 02, the adjustment is 0.01.

The sum of the prime rate, the adjustment for profitability, and the adjustment for experience is $m$, the assumed private opportunity cost of public debt replaced with private debt. In the example, $m$ is 11 percent in the first two years and 10 percent in the third year (line Hm of table A.1).

## What Is the Price of Private Equity?

Equity costs more than debt because equity is riskier. Benjamin (1994) estimates the price of private equity $M$ by adding a premium for risk to the price of private debt $m$.

Leverage $L$ is the ratio of liabilities to equity. As a DFI has more leverage, owners demand a higher Return on Equity (Modigliani and Miller 1958). More debt with a constant amount of equity means more fixed obligations and thus a higher risk to equity if revenues fall short. A bankrupt firm pays creditors before shareholders, so shareholders bear more risk as a DFI uses more debt. The example DFI does not have much leverage, ranging from 0.36 to 0.48 (line Hr of table A.1).

Based on historical data on leverage and ROE in the United States, Benjamin (1994) related $M$, the private opportunity cost of equity, to $m$, the private opportunity cost of public debt, and to $L$, leverage:

$$M = m \cdot (1.1 + 0.1 \cdot L). \tag{A.1}$$

For example, a DFI without debt would need to pay $1.1 \cdot m$ to attract private capital. A DFI with a debt : equity ratio of 9 : 1 would need to pay $2 \cdot m$ to attract private capital. For the example DFI, $M$ in its first three years is 13 percent, 13 percent, and 11 percent (line Hs of table A.1). This is about two percentage points higher than $m$.

This framework provides general guidelines and does not substitute for the judgment and knowledge of the analyst. For most public DFIs, the risk of the loss of public support and the pure business risk of its untested financial and organizational technology may swamp the risk due to its financial leverage.

For the example DFI, table A.2 computes an SDI using the private opportunity cost. Thus, it measures costs not to society but to private investors. This private SDI is a measure of the increase in the yield on loans that, all else constant, would allow a DFI to show a profit and to compensate for the private opportunity cost of funds, assuming that all public funds were replaced by private funds. For society, the SDI was 1.00, 0.50, and 0.00 (line Cx of table 2.4). For a private entity, the SDI is 1.07, 0.57, and 0.02 (line Ix of table A.2).

# Table A.2. Subsidy Dependence Index with Private Opportunity Costs

| Line | | | 12/31/01 | 12/31/02 | 12/31/03 |
|------|------|------|------|------|------|
| Ia | Start equity | $Al_{t-1} + Am_{t-1} + An_{t-1}$ | 0 | 2,200 | 3,100 |
| Ib | End equity | $Al + Am + An$ | 2,200 | 3,100 | 4,600 |
| Ic | Average equity, $E$ | $(Ia + Ib)/2$ | 1,100 | 2,650 | 3,850 |
| Id | Opportunity costs of private entities, $M$ | $Hs$ | 0.13 | 0.13 | 0.11 |
| Ie | Subsidy on equity, $E \cdot M$ | $Ic \cdot Id$ | 138 | 333 | 427 |
| If | Start public debt | $Aj_{t-1}$ | 0 | 400 | 800 |
| Ig | End public debt | $Aj$ | 400 | 800 | 1,200 |
| Ih | Average public debt, $A$ | $(If + Ig)/2$ | 200 | 600 | 1,000 |
| Ii | Exp. int. public debt, $A \cdot c$ | $Bf$ | 10 | 30 | 50 |
| Ij | Rate paid for public debt, $c$ | $Ii/Ih$ | 0.05 | 0.05 | 0.05 |
| Ik | Opportunity cost public debt, $m$ | $Hm$ | 0.11 | 0.11 | 0.10 |
| Il | Discount public debt, $A \cdot (m - c)$ | $Ih \cdot (Ik - Ij)$ | 12 | 36 | 47 |
| Im | Revenue grants, $RG$ | $Bl$ | 400 | 400 | 400 |
| In | Discounts on expenses, $DX$ | $Bn$ | 100 | 100 | 100 |

| | | | | | |
|---|---|---|---|---|---|
| Io | $K$ | Im + In | 500 | 500 | 500 |
| Ip | Accounting profit, $P$ | Bm | 200 | 255 | 935 |
| Iq | Subsidy, $S$ | Ie + Il + Io − Ip | 450 | 614 | 39 |
| Ir | Start loan portfolio (net) | $Ad_{t-1}$ | 0 | 2,100 | 3,300 |
| Is | End loan portfolio (net) | Ad | 2,100 | 3,300 | 5,200 |
| It | Average loan portfolio (net), $LP$ | (Ir + Is)/2 | 1,050 | 2,700 | 4,250 |
| Iu | Revenue from loans, $LP \cdot i$ | Ba | 420 | 1,080 | 1,700 |
| Iv | Yield on lending, $i$ | Iu/It | 0.40 | 0.40 | 0.40 |
| Iw | Revenue from lending, $LP \cdot i$ | It · Iv | 420 | 1,080 | 1,700 |
| Ix | Subsidy Dependence Index, SDI | Iq/Iw | 1.07 | 0.57 | 0.02 |
| Iy | Yield on lending, $i$ | Iv | 0.40 | 0.40 | 0.40 |
| Iz | Change in yield | Iy · Ix | 0.43 | 0.23 | 0.01 |
| Iaa | Subsidy-free yield | Iy + Iz | 0.83 | 0.63 | 0.41 |

*Note:* Monetary figures in constant units. Average equity includes profit in current period.
*Source:* Example of authors.

# References

Adams, Dale W. 1988. "The Conundrum of Successful Credit Projects in Floundering Rural Financial Markets." *Economic Development and Cultural Change* 36 (2) : 355–68.

Adams, Dale W, and J. D. Von Pischke. 1992. "Microenterprise Credit Programs: Déjà Vu." *World Development* 20 (10) : 1463–70.

Adams, Dale W, Douglas H. Graham, and J. D. Von Pischke. 1984. *Undermining Rural Development with Cheap Credit.* Boulder, Colo.: Westview.

Amin, Sajeda, Ashok S. Rai, and Giorgio Topa. 1999. "Does Microcredit Reach the Poor and Vulnerable? Evidence from Northern Bangladesh." Center for International Development Working Paper 28. Harvard University, Cambridge, Mass.

Ballard, Charles, John Shoven, and John Whalley. 1985. "General Equilibrium Computations of the Marginal Welfare Cost of Taxes in the United States." *American Economic Review* 75 (1) : 128–38.

Barltrop, Chris J., and Diana McNaughton. 1992. *Banking Institutions in Developing Markets.* Vol. 2: *Interpreting Financial Statements.* Washington, D.C.: World Bank.

Belli, Pedro. 1996a. *Handbook on Economic Analysis of Investment Operations.* Washington, D.C.: World Bank.

_____. 1996b. "Measurement of Sustainability." Memorandum to Orlando Sacay, October 9, World Bank, Washington, D.C.

Benjamin, McDonald P., Jr. 1994. "Credit Schemes for Microenterprises: Motivation, Design, and Viability." Ph.D. diss. Georgetown University, Washington, D.C.

Besley, Timothy. 1994. "How Do Market Failures Justify Intervention in Rural Credit Markets?" *World Bank Research Observer* 9 (1) : 27–47.

Binswanger, Hans P., and Shahidur R. Khandker. 1995. "The Impact of Formal Finance on the Rural Economy of India." *Journal of Development Studies* 32 (2) : 234–62.

Bolnick, Bruce R. 1988. "Evaluating Loan Collection Performance: An Indonesian Example." *World Development* 16 (4) : 501–10.

Bolnick, Bruce R., and Eric R. Nelson. 1990. "Evaluating the Economic Impact of a Special Credit Programme: KIK/KMKP in Indonesia." *Journal of Development Studies* 26 (2) : 299–312.

Brent, Robert J. 1996. *Applied Cost-Benefit Analysis.* Cheltenham: Edward Elgar.

Brigham, Eugene F., and Louis C. Gapenski. 1993. *Intermediate Financial Management.* Fort Worth: Dryden.

Buckley, Graeme. 1997. "Microfinance in Africa: Is It Either the Problem or the Solution?" *World Development* 25 (7) : 1081–93.

Carter, Michael R. 1989. "The Impact of Credit on Peasant Productivity and Differentiation in Nicaragua." *Journal of Development Economics* 31 : 13–36.

Carter, Michael R., and Pedro Olinto. 1996. "Getting Institutions Right for Whom? The Wealth-Differentiated Impact of Property Rights Reform on Investment and Income in Rural Paraguay." University of Wisconsin—Madison. Processed.

Chaves, Rodrigo A., and Claudio Gonzalez-Vega. 1996. "The Design of Successful Rural Financial Intermediaries: Evidence from Indonesia." *World Development* 24 (1) : 65–78.

Christen, Robert Peck. 1997. *Banking Services for the Poor: Managing for Financial Success: An Expanded and Revised Guidebook for Development Finance Institutions.* Boston: Acción International.

Christen, Robert Peck, Elisabeth Rhyne, Robert C. Vogel, and Cressida McKean. 1995. "Maximizing the Outreach of Microenterprise Finance: An Analysis of Successful Microfinance Programs." Program and Operations Assessment Report 10. United States Agency for International Development, Washington, D.C.

Coleman, Brett E. 1999. "The Impact of Group Lending in Northeast Thailand." *Journal of Development Economics* 60 : 105–41.

Conrad, Douglas A. 1984. "Returns on Equity to Not-for-Profit Hospitals: Theory and Implementation." *Health Services Research* 19 (1) : 42–63.

_____. 1986. "Returns on Equity for Not-for-Profit Hospitals: A Commentary and Elaboration." *Health Services Research* 21 (1) : 17–20.

Dasgupta, Ajit K., and D. W. Pearce. 1978. *Cost-Benefit Analysis: The Theory and Practice.* London: Macmillan.

David, Cristina C., and Richard L. Meyer. 1983. "Measuring the Farm Level Impact of Agricultural Loans." In J. D. Von Pischke, Dale W Adams, and Gordon Donald, eds., *Rural Financial Markets in Developing Countries.* Baltimore: Johns Hopkins University Press.

Devarajan, Shantayanan, Lyn Squire, and Sethaput Suthiwart-Narueput. 1997. "Beyond Rate of Return: Reorienting Project Appraisal." *World Bank Research Observer* 12 (1) : 35–46.

*The Economist.* 1997. "Valuing Companies: a Star to Sail By?" August 1 : 53–55.

Feder, Gershon, Laurence J. Lau, Justin Y. Lin, and Xiapeng Luo. 1990. "The Relationship between Credit and Productivity in Chinese Agriculture: A Microeconomic Model of Disequilibrium." *American Journal of Agricultural Economics* 72 (5) : 1152–57.

Gale, William G. 1991. "Economic Effects of Federal Credit Programs." *American Economic Review* 81 (1) : 33–52.

Garber, Alan M., and Charles E. Phelps. 1997. "Economic Foundations of Cost-Effectiveness Analysis." *Journal of Health Economics* 16 : 1–31.

Gittinger, J. Price. 1982. *Economic Analysis of Agricultural Projects.* Baltimore: Johns Hopkins University Press.

Goldschmidt, Yaaqov. 1992. "International Accounting Standard 29: Formulation and Clarification of Income Measurement in Hyperinflationary Economies." *International Journal of Accounting* 27 : 137–50.

Goldschmidt, Yaaqov, and Jacob Yaron. 1991. "Inflation Adjustment of Financial Statements: Application of International Accounting Standard 29." Working Paper 670. World Bank, Washington, D.C.

Goldschmidt, Yaaqov, Leon Shashua, and Jimmye S. Hillman. 1986. *The Impact of Inflation on Financial Activity in Business with Applications to the U.S. Farming Sector.* Lanham, Md.: Rowman and Littlefield.

Gonzalez-Vega, Claudio. 1998. "Microfinance Apex Mechanisms: Concepts, Synthesis of Lessons, and Recommendations." Report to the Consultative Group to Assist the Poorest. Ohio State University, Columbus.

Gonzalez-Vega, Claudio, Mark Schreiner, Richard L. Meyer, Jorge Rodriguez-Meza, and Sergio Navajas. 1997. "BancoSol: The Challenge of Growth for Microfinance Organizations." In Hartmut Schneider, ed., *Microfinance for the Poor?* Paris: OECD (Organisation for Economic Co-operation and Development).

Hashemi, Syed M. 1997. "Building up Capacity for Banking with the Poor: The Grameen Bank of Bangladesh." In Hartmut Schneider, ed., *Microfinance for the Poor?* Paris: OECD.

Heckman, James J., and Jeffrey A. Smith. 1995. "Assessing the Case for Social Experiments." *Journal of Economic Perspectives* 9 (2) : 85–110.

Helms, Brigit S. 1997. "Anatomy of a Micro-Finance Deal: The New Approach to Investing in Micro-Finance Institutions." Consultative Group to Assist the Poorest Focus Note 9. World Bank, Washington, D.C.

_____. 1998. "Cost Allocation for Multi-Service Microfinance Institutions." Consultative Group to Assist the Poorest Occasional Paper 2. World Bank, Washington, D.C.

Holtmann, Martin, and Rochus Mommartz. 1996. *Technical Guide for Analyzing the Efficiency of Credit-Granting Non-Government Organizations (NGOs).* Saarbrücken: Breitenbach.

Hossain, Mahabub. 1988. "Credit for Alleviation of Rural Poverty: The Grameen Bank in Bangladesh." Research Report 65. International Food Policy Research Institute, Washington, D.C.

Hulme, David, and Paul Mosley. 1996. *Finance Against Poverty*, Vols. I and II. London: Routledge.

IADB (Inter-American Development Bank). 1994. *Technical Guide for the Analysis of Microenterprise Finance Institutions.* Washington, D.C.

IMF (International Monetary Fund). Various years. *International Financial Statistics*. Washington, D.C.

Iqbal, Farrukh. 1986. "The Demand and Supply of Funds among Agricultural Households in India." In Inderjit Singh, Lyn Squire, and John Strauss, eds., *Agricultural Household Models*. Baltimore: Johns Hopkins University Press.

Jennings, Edward H. 1993. "Financial Management in Not-for-Profit Businesses." In Eugene F. Brigham and Louis C. Gapenski, eds., *Intermediate Financial Management*. Fort Worth: Dryden.

Katz, David A., and H. Gilbert Welch. 1993. "Discounting in Cost-Effectiveness Analysis of Healthcare Programmes." *PharmacoEconomics* 3 (4) : 276–285.

Khandker, Shahidur R. 1996. "Grameen Bank: Impact, Costs, and Program Sustainability." *Asian Development Review* 14 (1) : 97–130.

Khandker, Shahidur R., and Baqui Khalily. 1996. "The Bangladesh Rural Advancement Committee's Credit Programs: Performance and Sustainability." World Bank Discussion Paper 324. Washington, D.C.

Khandker, Shahidur R., Baqui Khalily, and Zahed Khan. 1995. "Grameen Bank: Performance and Sustainability." World Bank Discussion Paper 306. Washington, D.C.

Khandker, Shahidur R., Zahed Khan, and Baqui Khalily. 1995. "Sustainability of a Government Targeted Credit Program: Evidence from Bangladesh." World Bank Discussion Paper 316. Washington, D.C.

Koch, Timothy W. 1992. *Bank Management*. Fort Worth: Dryden.

Krahnen, Jan Pieter, and Reinhard H. Schmidt. 1994. *Development Finance as Institution Building*. Boulder, Colo.: Westview.

Ladman, Jerry R., and Ronald L. Tinnermeier. 1981. "The Political Economy of Agricultural Credit: The Case of Bolivia." *American Journal of Agricultural Economics* 62 : 66–72.

Lapar, Ma. Lucila A., Douglas H. Graham, Richard L. Meyer, and David S. Kraybill. 1995. "Selectivity Bias in Estimating the Effect of Credit on

Output: The Case of Rural Nonfarm Enterprises in the Philippines." Economics and Sociology Occasional Paper 2231. Ohio State University, Columbus.

Lipton, Michael, and Martin Ravallion. 1995. "Poverty and Policy." In Jere Behrman and T. N. Srinivasan, eds., *Handbook of Development Economics.* Vol. IIIB. Amsterdam: Elsevier.

Markandya, Anil, and David W. Pearce. 1991. "Development, the Environment, and the Social Rate of Discount." *World Bank Research Observer* 6 (2) : 137–52.

McKernan, Signe-Mary. 1996. "The Impact of Micro-Credit Programs on Self-Employment Profits: Do Non-Credit Program Aspects Matter? Essays on Micro-Credit Programs: The Grameen Bank Experience." Ph.D. diss. Brown University, Providence, R.I.

McKnelly, Barbara, and Christopher Dunford. 1998. *Impact of Credit with Education on Mothers' and Their Young Children's Nutrition: Lower Pra Rural Bank Credit with Education Program in Ghana.* Davis, Calif.: Freedom from Hunger.

Mishan, E. J. 1988. *Cost-Benefit Analysis.* New York: Praeger.

Modigliani, F., and M. Miller. 1958. "The Cost of Capital, Corporation Finance, and the Theory of Investment." *American Economic Review* 49 (2) : 261–97.

Moffitt, Robert. 1991. "Program Evaluation with Nonexperimental Data." *Evaluation Review* 15 (3) : 291–314.

Montgomery, Mark, Terry Johnson, and Syed Faisal. 2000. "Who Succeeds at Starting a Business? Evidence from the Washington Self-Employment Demonstration." Grinnell College, Grinnell, Iowa. Processed.

Morduch, Jonathan.1998. "Does Microfinance Really Help the Poor? New Evidence from Flagship Programs in Bangladesh." Princeton University, Princeton, N.J. Processed.

_____. 1999. "The Role of Subsidies in Microfinance: Evidence from the Grameen Bank." *Journal of Development Economics* 60: 229–48.

_____. 2000. "The Microfinance Schism." *World Development* 28 (4) : 617–29.

Mosley, Paul. 1996. "Metamorphosis from NGO to Commercial Bank: The Case of BancoSol in Bolivia." In David Hulme and Paul Mosley, eds., *Finance Against Poverty.* Vol. II. London: Routledge.

Mosley, Paul, and David Hulme. 1998. "Microenterprise Finance: Is There a Conflict between Growth and Poverty Alleviation?" *World Development* 26 (5) : 783–90.

Mould, Maurice C. 1987. *Financial Information for Management of a Development Finance Institution.* World Bank Technical Paper 63, Industry and Finance Series. Washington, D.C.

Norgaard, Richard B., and Richard B. Howarth. 1992. "Sustainability and Intergenerational Environmental Rights: Implications for Benefit-Cost Analysis." In John M. Reilly and Margot Anderson, eds., *Economic Issues in Global Climate Change: Agriculture, Forestry, and Natural Resources.* Boulder, Colo.: Westview.

Pauly, Mark V. 1986. "Returns on Equity for Not-for-Profit Hospitals." *Health Services Research* 21 (1) : 1–16.

Paxton, Julia. 1996. *A Worldwide Inventory of Microfinance Institutions.* Washington, D.C.: World Bank.

Pitt, Mark M., and Shahidur R. Khandker. 1998. "The Impact of Group-Based Credit Programs on Poor Households in Bangladesh: Does the Gender of the Participants Matter?" *Journal of Political Economy* 106 (5) : 958–96.

Quirk, James, and Katsuaki Terasawa. 1991. "Choosing a Government Discount Rate: An Alternative Approach." *Journal of Environmental Economics and Management* 20 : 16–28.

RESULTS International. 1996. "The Microcredit Summit Declaration and Plan of Action." *Journal of Developmental Entrepreneurship* 1 (2) : 131–76.

Richardson, David C. 1994. "PEARLS: Financial Stabilization, Monitoring, and Evaluation." Research Monograph Series 4. World Council of Credit Unions, Madison, Wis.

Rogaly, Ben. 1996. "Micro-Finance Evangelism, 'Destitute Women,' and the Hard Selling of a New Anti-Poverty Formula." *Development in Practice* 6 (2) : 100–12.

Rosenberg, Richard. 1994. "Beyond Self-Sufficiency: Licensed Leverage and Microfinance Strategy." USAID (U. S. Agency for International Development) Microenterprise Development Brief 17, Washington, D.C. Processed.

_____. 1996. "Microcredit Interest Rates." Consultative Group to Assist the Poorest Occasional Paper 1. World Bank, Washington, D.C. Processed.

Rosenberg, Richard, Robert Peck Christen, and Brigit Helms. 1997. "Format for Appraisal of Micro-Finance Institutions." Consultative Group to Assist the Poorest Technical Tools Series 4. World Bank, Washington, D.C. Processed.

Sacay, Orlando. 1996. "Measuring Subsidy and Sustainability of Microfinance Institutions." World Bank, Washington, D.C. Processed.

Sacay, O., B. Randhawa, and M. Agabin. 1996. "The BAAC Success Story: A Specialized Agriculture Bank under Government Ownership." World Bank, Washington, D.C. Processed.

Schmidt, Reinhard H. 1997. "Corporate Governance: The Role of Other Constituencies." In Alice Pezard and Jean-Marie Thiveaud, eds., *Corporate Governance: Les Perspectives Internationales*. Paris: Association d'Economie Financière.

Schmidt, Reinhard, and Claus-Peter Zeitinger. 1996. "The Efficiency of Credit-Granting NGOs in Latin America." *Savings and Development* 20 (3) : 353–84.

Schreiner, Mark. 1995. "Meta-rules." Economics and Sociology Occasional Paper 2268. Ohio State University, Columbus.

_____. 1997. "A Framework for the Analysis of the Performance and Sustainability of Subsidized Microfinance Organizations with Application to BancoSol of Bolivia and Grameen Bank of Bangladesh." Ph.D. diss. Ohio State University, Columbus.

_____. 1999a. *Aspects of Outreach: A Framework for the Discussion of the Social Benefits of Microfinance*. Center for Social Development Working Paper 99-3. Washington University in St. Louis.

_____. 1999b. "A Cost-Effectiveness Analysis of the Grameen Bank of Bangladesh." Center for Social Development Working Paper 99-5. Washington University in St. Louis.

98 DEVELOPMENT FINANCE INSTITUTIONS

_____. 2000a. "A Framework for Financial Benefit-Cost Analysis of Individual Development Accounts at the Experimental Site of the American Dream Demonstration." Center for Social Development, Washington University in St. Louis. Processed.

_____. 2000b. "Resources Used in 1998 and 1999 to Produce Individual Development Accounts in the Experimental Program of the American Dream Demonstration at the Community Action Project of Tulsa County." Center for Social Development, Washington University in St. Louis. Processed.

SEEP. 1995. *Financial Ratio Analysis of Micro-Finance Institutions.* New York: Pact.

Sherraden, Michael. 1991. *Assets and the Poor: A New American Welfare Policy.* Armonk, N.Y.: M. E. Sharpe.

Sherraden, Michael, Lissa Johnson, Margaret Clancy, Sondra Beverly, Mark Schreiner, Min Zhan, and Jami Curley. 2000. "Savings Patterns in IDA Programs—Downpayments on the American Dream Policy Demonstration, a National Demonstration of Individual Development Accounts." Center for Social Development, Washington University in St. Louis.

Sial, Maqbool H., and Michael R. Carter. 1996. "Financial Market Efficiency in an Agrarian Economy: Microeconometric Analysis of the Pakistani Punjab." *Journal of Development Studies* 32 (5) : 771–98.

Silvers, J. B., and Robert T. Kauer. 1986. "Returns on Equity for Not-for-Profit Hospitals: Some Comments." *Health Services Research* 21 (1) : 21–28.

Singh, Inderjit, Lyn Squire, and John Strauss. 1986. "A Survey of Agricultural Household Models: Recent Findings and Policy Implications." *World Bank Economic Review* 1 (1) : 149–79.

Smith, Stephen C., and Sanjay Jain. 1998. "Village Banking and Maternal and Child Health: Theory and Preliminary Evidence from Honduras and Ecuador." George Washington University, Washington, D.C. Processed.

Stickney, Clyde P., and Roman L. Weil. 1994. *Financial Accounting: An Introduction to Concepts, Methods, and Uses.* Fort Worth: Dryden.

Stiglitz, Joseph E. 1993. "The Role of the State in Financial Markets." In *Proceedings of the World Bank Annual Conference on Development Economics 1993*. Washington, D.C.: World Bank.

_____. 1998. "The Private Uses of Public Interests: Incentives and Institutions." *Journal of Economic Perspectives* 12 (2) : 3–22.

Stiglitz, Joseph E., and Andrew Weiss. 1981. "Credit Rationing in Markets with Imperfect Information." *American Economic Review* 71 : 393–410.

Tollison, R. 1984. "Politics without Romance: A Sketch of Positive Public Choice Theory and Its Normative Implications." In R. Tollison and J. Buchanan, eds., *The Theory of Public Choice–II*. Ann Arbor: University of Michigan Press.

Tully, Shawn. 1993. "The Real Key to Creating Wealth." *Fortune*, September 20, pp. 143, 160–2.

_____. 1994. "America's Best Wealth Creators." *Fortune*, November 28, pp. 38–50.

Tweeten, Luther. 1992. *Agricultural Trade: Principles and Policies*. Boulder, Colo.: Westview.

Von Pischke, J. D. 1991. *Finance at the Frontier: Debt Capacity and the Role of Credit in the Private Economy*. Washington, D.C.: World Bank.

_____. 1996. "Measuring the Trade-Off between Outreach and Sustainability of Microenterprise Lenders." *Journal of International Development* 8 (2) : 225–39.

_____. 1998. "Measuring the Performance of Small Enterprise Lenders." In Mwangi S. Kimeny, Robert C. Wieland, and J. D. Von Pischke, eds., *Strategic Issues in Microfinance*. Brookfield: Avebury.

Von Pischke, J. D. and Dale W Adams. 1980. "Fungibility and the Design and Evaluation of Agricultural Credit Projects." *American Journal of Agricultural Economics* 62 : 719–24

Von Pischke, J. D., Robert C. Vogel, Peter Flath, and Maurice C. Mould. 1988. "Measurement of Loan Repayment Performance." Economic Development Institute Course Note 030/086. World Bank, Washington, D.C.

Weinstein, Milton C., and William B. Stason. 1977. "Foundations of Cost-Effectiveness Analysis for Health and Medical Practices." *New England Journal of Medicine* 296 (13) : 716–21.

Wheeler, John R. C., and Jan P. Clement. 1990. "Capital Expenditure Decisions and the Role of the Not-for-Profit Hospital: An Application of a Social Goods Model." *Medical Care Review* 47 (4) : 467–86.

Women's World Banking. 1995. "The Missing Links: Financial Systems that Work for the Majority." New York. Processed.

World Bank. 1989. *World Development Report 1989: Financial Systems and Development.* New York: Oxford University Press.

_____. 1994. "Mexico: Agricultural Sector Memorandum." World Bank, Natural Resources and Poverty Division and Latin America and Caribbean Regional Office, Country Department II, Washington, D.C.

Yaron, Jacob. 1992a. *Successful Rural Finance Institutions.* World Bank Discussion Paper 150. Washington, D.C.

_____. 1992b. *Assessing Development Finance Institutions: A Public Interest Analysis.* World Bank Discussion Paper 174. Washington, D.C.

_____. 1994. "What Makes Rural Finance Institutions Successful?" *World Bank Research Observer* 9 (9) : 49–70.

Yaron, Jacob, McDonald Benjamin, and Gerda Piprek. 1997. *Rural Finance: Issues, Design, and Best Practices.* Environmentally Sustainable Development Studies and Monographs Series 14. World Bank, Washington, D.C.

www.ingramcontent.com/pod-product-compliance
Lightning Source LLC
Chambersburg PA
CBHW031521270326
41930CB00006B/468

*  9 7 8 0 8 2 1 3 4 9 8 4 7  *